Presented to

_____

From

_____

Date

_____

ELLIE'VATION

Advance praise for Ellie'vation

"I recommend this book to anyone who may struggle with feeling that they have messed up too often or too much and think God has given up on them. Be encouraged! He has not and never will! I was Ellie'vated in my own heart......Truth is, this was a 'word' I needed and I'm grateful for."

~ Carl Tuttle, Pastor, Songwriter, Vineyard Worship – The Early Years, Author of Reckless Mercy: A Trophy of God's Grace. California, USA.

"Like fresh manna from heaven, Ellie'vation is masterfully and beautifully written, full of wise counsel, filled with life-changing applications and is simply a blessing to read."

Pastor Ruth Loisa M. Maglaya, Send the Light Ministries, Philippines.

"Ellie has been a good friend of mine for several years. After every conversation I have ever had with her I always come away lifted and encouraged! As I read Ellie'vation I had the same feelings I get from our warm conversations. In this day and time we all need the messages in this book from God's heart to ours."

Reyna Little, Broadcaster and Producer – News Peace Podcast – www.YouTube.com/reyna4321 Texas, USA.

"Ellie will definitely keep you Ellie'vated as you flick through the extensive God given revelations each day. This easy to read book will draw you closer to the heart of God and reveal His heart for you. You'll also get a close up view of the heart of the author."

Revd Bishop Ann Laidlow, The Dream Centre, Alicante, Spain.

"A deeply personal exploration of faith that is accessible, engaging, and universal......A book you'll read again and again and carry with you. It breathes life into belief, and belief into life!"

Mohamedou Ould Salahi, Author of The Mauritanian (the book that inspired the movie),
Speaker and Life Coach.

"Ellie'vation is an inspirational and encouraging tool that everyone can use to feed into their daily life. The words narrate thoughts and feelings that most readers would have experienced at some point……..and help to put scenarios into perspective…….. this book allows hope to rise and reign!"

Leanne Ajadi-Burke, Empowerment Coach
Derby, UK. www.leannejaneajadi.com

"This is an excellent, authentic perspective of Ellie's relationship with Jesus, written with personal experiences, passion, and displaying Biblical truths."

Pastor Chris Jones, Kings Church Blackpool,
UK.

"I have known Ellie for many years and when she told me she was writing another book I had high expectations. Ellie'vation has truly managed to surpass my very high expectations! Ellie shows you that through the love of God anything is achievable and reachable! Truly inspiring and motivating."

Pritpal Singh Makan, Senior Chaplain – HMPPS.
SSO, Manchester, UK.

"*As I started reading, one of my most favourite things to happen, happened! God renewed my mind in how I think of Him again! Ellie has a beautiful way of bringing the reader back into the right perspective of His nature and His ways. This is a book I'd pick up again and again."*

Rebekah Waring, Worship Leader, Singer/Songwriter – **Rise Up Warrior** Album
Preston, UK.

Ellie Palma-Cass

ELLIE'VATION

Lifting You Up Above Your Situation

Ellie'vation – Lifting You Up Above Your Situation
Copyright © 2022

Ellie Palma-Cass has asserted her right under the Copyright, Designs and Patents Act, 1988, to be identified as the author of this work.

First published by KDP in 2022

All rights reserved. No part of this publication may be reproduced, stored in a retrieval system, or transmitted in any form or by any means – electronic, mechanical, digital, photocopy, recording, or any other – except for brief quotations in printed reviews, without the prior permission of the author.
Contact info@elliepalmacass.com
www.elliepalmacass.com

Book cover and editing by The Write Companion
www.thewritecompanion.co.uk

Illustrations by Philippa Kay.

Unless otherwise indicated, all Scripture quotations are taken from NKJV

Contents

DAY 1: WHAT DO YOU WANT TO CHANGE?...................17
DAY 2: WHAT SHALL WE WEAR TODAY?.....................21
DAY 3: IDENTITY....... REAL?...........................25
DAY 4: DO YOU FEEL EXCITED? DO YOU FEEL PREPARED? ... 30
DAY 5: NOW, WHERE DID I PUT THOSE HIKING BOOTS?.........35
DAY 6: NOT EVERY TABLE IS GOD'S TABLE..................40
DAY 7: LOOK AT WHAT CAN HAPPEN!.......................44
DAY 8: ENCOURAGE YOURSELF!............................47
DAY 9: THERE'S NO NEED TO SEE BEYOND THE BEND..........51
DAY 10: WALK DOWN THIS NEW PATH.......................55
DAY 11: GET BACK UP! 60
DAY 12: WHY DID IT TAKE SO LONG?......................63
DAY 13: IT'S NEVER TOO LATE!..........................68
DAY 14: PURSUE THOSE GOALS............................72
DAY 15: ANYTHING CAN HAPPEN!..........................77
DAY 16: WHY, THANK YOU!...............................80
DAY 17: I'VE GOT THE POWER!...........................84
DAY 18: NONE OF US ARE PERFECT........................87
DAY 19: EVERYBODY HURTS......SOMETIMES................91
DAY 20: HE IS BIG! 96
DAY 21: THERE IS NO COMPARISON!.......................99
DAY 22: HEALTH AND SAFETY............................102
DAY 23: IT'S ALL TIED TOGETHER.......................106

DAY 24: THE MEASURE OF YOUR COMPASSION 109
DAY 25: WE NEED TO TALK ABOUT FORGIVENESS 113
DAY 26: WE STILL NEED TO TALK ABOUT FORGIVENESS 117
DAY 27: IT'S NONE OF YOUR BUSINESS..120
DAY 28: I SMILE 124
DAY 29: THIS TOO SHALL PASS 129
DAY 30: DON'T LOOK BACK 132
DAY 31: FIND YOUR TRIBE 135
DAY 32: IT'S NEVER TOO LATE...138
DAY 33: WHAT DO YOU SEE?..142
DAY 34: WHO ARE YOU LISTENING TO? 145
DAY 35: TINY ACTION – HUGE IMPACT 148
DAY 36: THE BEST DEFENCE 152
DAY 37: DID YOU CHECK THE OIL AND WATER? 155
DAY 38: SPLIT SECOND THOUGHTS – LIFELONG MEMORIES
....159
DAY 39: LET IT GO 165
DAY 40: CELEBRATE BRAVERY 168

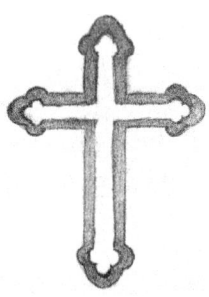

Foreword

Ellie'vation daily devotional is truly unlike any other!

For 40 days you can experience gems of wisdom from Ellie's own authentic and raw life journey. Her words are gentle yet challenging, reassuring yet still propelling the reader out of complacency and into fruitful action.

This little book offers the reader a path of deeper self-reflection, revealing our fears and insecurities, showing us who we truly are and more importantly, what is stopping us from becoming who we have been made to be. However, Ellie doesn't stop there, but always goes on to lift the reader's gaze to the practical, spiritual, mental, emotional, and even physical strategies to reaching complete wholeness and Ellie'vation! This book extends the opportunity for the reader to 'make their comeback', to get up from defeat and to walk into lasting victory through the hope that Jesus brings.

Ellie'vation will shift your perspective with a truth everlasting. Ellie's stories from her own life bring a radical sense of familiarity and comfort, while her perfectly appropriate use of scripture will fill your heart and mind with a confidence and hope that is so much bigger than anything you may be facing. She highlights the powerful, unchanging truth of scripture to the ups and downs of life, bringing profound yet accessible revelation.

Ellie offers her reader the opportunity to start every day with a peace that is not dictated by circumstance, whilst creating space for deeply productive personal reflection our busy lives simply could never offer.

This book will change your life if you allow it to. Grab hold of the opportunity to Ellie'vate every aspect of your life, and you will see and experience Jesus through Ellie's personal testimony and through the scriptures you read. You will come fully awake and alive, perhaps for the first time!

Susanna Raj
New Beginning Church
Preston, UK

Note from Ellie

What is it about the number 40? We find that when it is referred to in the Bible it's usually connected to times of testing, a time of pushing through, a time of pressing in, a time of overcoming. At the end of the 40 days is the triumph, or the lesson, or the victory.

I wanted to produce a devotional for 40 days because I have found that whenever I commit to this time period for anything, whether it be a time of fasting something, or waiting for something, there is always a transformation at the end. Either a small character transformation in me; I learn something new about myself, I climb another spiritual level, or a complete renewal in my outer circle. Something changes when we commit to growth, when we execute improvement in our lives, spiritually and emotionally.

It doesn't even have to be a big, powerful event either. A small, insignificant statement can spark a detonation of emotion in someone, a healing can begin deep inside, and we discover at the end of the 40 days our life has changed and we didn't even know it needed to!

I was guided by the Holy Spirit as I wrote. Some of the devotions are long, some are short, but I hope they, and the study of the Scriptures laid out, touch some part of you that needs to Ellie'vate as you travel with me on this 40 day journey.

The Ellie'vation's at the end of the devotionals may seem insignificant little acts, but I have come to find that in life, it's the little things, the simple changes, that have made the biggest impact, opened the most unusual doors, and set up some of the most wonderful chain reactions.

Be Ellie'vated!

With love,

Ellie

Dedication

To my incredible daughter, Rhiannon, who Ellie'vates every part of my life!

I love you more, I love you most, and I am so proud of you.

To Stella, my best friend, our star, we love you, we miss you, we will never forget you.

Day One

What do you want to change?

Is there some part of your life that needs change?

Are you believing for change but you're so comfortable where you are that deep down you know the change won't happen? And is it really *comfort* that is keeping you where you are or is it fear of the unknown?

There is an old saying, 'Change is the only constant, so learn to embrace it' and I have found that to be true in my life. I adapt very well to change but I acknowledge that for some people change is anathema!

However, I fundamentally believe that change isn't really the issue.

Fear is.

Fear of not knowing what is ahead. Anxiety about taking the wrong direction. Despair that you may never be as snug as a bug in a rug again!

I am always astonished that Joshua and Caleb, in the book of Joshua, were the only ones who believed they could take the land of Canaan, even though God had *already* promised the Israelites that the land was theirs. It was their 'Promised Land!' Yet, because it didn't look like it, and because they were comfortable, and because they were fearful of *change*, they were willing to forfeit their PROMISE from God!

Today I want to Ellie'vate your mood, your countenance, your day, by reminding you who you are and how to speak life! If you know the living God, if you have a relationship with Jesus, then you know that you are the son or daughter of a King, you know that you are a warrior, a soldier on the frontline, a human being who is on this earth for a short time eternally speaking, but someone who, when in need, can call on a great big God!

If you want or need to change something, step out in faith! And begin!

Fear must bow down to faith!

When God sees you stepping out in faith, knowing that you're a little apprehensive but you're doing it anyway, He says, "The Lord is with you, mighty warrior," or "The Lord is with you, mighty warrior princess." Just like the time He looked down on His servant Gideon. You can read his story in Judges 6. Gideon was a blithering wreck, yet God saw him as a mighty warrior!

So, what do you want to change?

A great way to begin to Ellie'vate your day is to SPEAK out and DECLARE truth over you and your life!

Change the way you speak about yourself and to yourself! We're often told about the negative effect it has on a person when they are labelled, but I have noticed so many people label themselves! Don't do it! If you allow it, without exception, your mind is determined to highlight your flaws and the blunders you've made, and it can lead you to a miserable place. Why do you think God said, "………**whatever things**

are true, whatever things are noble, whatever things are just, whatever things are pure, whatever things are lovely, whatever things are of good report ...... meditate (consider, ruminate, ponder) on these things." Philippians 4:8

God knows that a pessimistic outlook coupled with pitiful speech can be downright dangerous for you. Your mind absorbs negative information easily and it's been proven that this is the case!

If you keep telling yourself unkind things about yourself, i.e., "I'll never be any good at singing," or, "I'll never be as happy as my neighbour," and so on, whatever negative comments make you feel miserable, then a gush in activity in a critical data processing area of the brain happens and this can start to drain your energy resulting in you feeling literally drained! That's why we need to build ourselves up and SPEAK LIFE over our lives, our day, our loved ones.

Believe that even the biggest giants you are facing in your life, in your day today can disappear when you speak out and believe! One thing I have discovered in my own life, is that however big my challenges are, however desperate my circumstances have felt, however depressing the diagnosis was, however bereft I felt when I experienced huge loss, when I spoke out the promises of God over my circumstances, things changed! Maybe not straight away, but things changed eventually. That's where your faith is grown. What is the point of faith if it's never tested? Anybody can say, "I have a deep faith in God," if they never need an answer to a prayer. Where is the proof of their faith?

Today change the words and proclamations that pour out of your mouth. Remember to speak life. Speak the promises of God which He gave to you in scripture.

Watch your day change.

Watch your life change.

Feel your mood Ellie'vate!

Read ~ Psalm 94:19, Proverbs 18:21, Romans 10:17

Ellie'vation ~ Listen to the song 'Goodness of God' by Bethel Music – sung by Jenn Johnson. Play it loud! And join in!

Day 2

What shall we wear today?

My daughter came out with a cracker of a comment recently! We were discussing the merits of being groomed and how to present yourself. I love to wear full make-up and I do enjoy putting outfits together. My daughter is the same, yet when we do 'slob out' as we call it, we are absolutely unrecognisable! We go from one extreme to another and this particular day we were having a discussion about randomly bumping into people and how we should always be prepared, ready, and groomed. My daughter said, "Well Mum, you know what God says!"

I replied, with eyebrows raised and in eager anticipation because I was genuinely wondering what God said about randomly bumping into people without make-up on, "What does He say?!"

"God says, 'Dress for the life you want!'"

Now, here is where I'd like to highlight the fact that my daughter reads her Bible and is in fact on fire for God! But I didn't even have to begin to tell her that God most definitely doesn't use that phrase in the Bible because the confusion on my face apparently said it all!

It did make me laugh though and friends point out my daughter is becoming more like her mum every day! I'll leave that right there.

But it got me thinking……Or should I say, as I sit here at my desk in front of my window on my laptop…….. I couldn't help but wonder…….

Does God tell us, in a roundabout way, to dress for the life we want?

When we read the Bible, we discover there isn't a dress code for us to follow. And I suppose that's a good job really! Because fashion has definitely changed over the years.

However, scripture does encourage us to place attention on arraying ourselves with good qualities and the fruits of the Holy Spirit. Shouldn't we be more concerned with dressing ourselves in the things of God? As I read more about this, I

noticed something. Whenever we are given the choice to be clothed in anything by our Lord, we always receive something more. Wow! There is always more with God! Always extra!

When we choose to 'put on humility' we then go on to receive His grace.

When we choose to 'put on the armour of God' we then are able to stand firm against the schemes of the devil.

When we choose to follow Jesus, He promises to 'clothe us with power from on high.'

When we choose to 'put on a heart of compassion, kindness, humility, gentleness and patience' this helps us to make allowances for others and to forgive thus we receive forgiveness too.

Everything we are advised to 'put on', everything we can clothe ourselves in, leads to us receiving something else to benefit our lives from God!

And for me, the life I truly, truly want, is a life filled with God's glory. A life filled with His love, His direction, His promises, His testimony. HIM!

So, yes! My daughter was right! In a roundabout way God does tell us to dress for the life we want! He provides the best garments, the most beautiful garments, the most protective garments.

To Ellie'vate yourself today, dress in THE top, most exclusive, designer's clothes.

Dress for the blessed life you want!

Read ~ 1 Peter 3:3-4, Isaiah 61:10, Revelation 3:5

Ellie'vation ~ Wear something different today; something you wouldn't normally wear. Try a new style. Put on a new shade of lipstick or jewellery that isn't your normal taste. Decide to wear a smile all day no matter what!

Day 3

Identity....... real?

Have you ever noticed the posters on social media which read 'A real man this' and 'A real woman that'. Apparently, if a man or a woman doesn't act a certain way or doesn't do a certain thing and it's not to somebody else's standard, it seems they're not real! Hmmm, maybe they just didn't get there yet......wherever 'there' is! Maybe these 'unreal' people are still at the learning part of that particular chapter in their journey. But we are ALL real, whether we get it right or wrong; every person on the planet is real!

We feel real emotions, real pain, real joy, real anger, real ecstasy; it's all real!

And the more I read the content of these posts, I see the almost desperate need to fit in! With other people's ideals??

But guess what?

When God decided you were going to be a person on this

earth and planned your place on His planet before even the foundations of the earth were formed, He already had a plan and a purpose for you! But it wasn't to fit in with any club, clique, group, or opinions of men! He didn't CALL you and CHOOSE you, for THEM! He called you and chose you for HIS purposes, all planned for you to undertake as His child; for HIS good, as well as your own.

BE GLAD if you don't fit in! You're not particularly meant to!

Now, I'm not saying it's not a beautiful thing to be part of a church or part of a ministry because we are definitely called to fellowship and to love one another as brothers and sisters.

Church is a huge part of my life and I believe we must find a church to be a part of. It's imperative to be with family. But don't put your faith in people; put your faith in God! People can and will, let you down, because like you and me they are human! But your identity isn't in people, it's in Christ!

A few weeks ago, I had my handbag stolen. I'm a woman! And my handbag was stolen! Everybody is well aware of the trauma of a woman suffering the loss of her handbag! But joking aside, I was very upset. Yes, there were cards, money, sunglasses, and shopping lists but the thing that caused me the most fear and worry at the time was the loss of my driving licence. My whole identity was on my driving licence, my name, address, date of birth and even my photograph! I felt completely vulnerable, and my concerns were that my identity would be stolen.

As I prayed that evening about the whole episode I felt such an immense peace. I felt God say to me, "Ellie, your identity

is in Me, and it can never be stolen. Not even the enemy himself can steal away your identity in Me."

"If then, you were raised with Christ, seek those things which are above, where Christ is, sitting at the right hand of God. Set your mind on things above, not on things on the earth. For you died, and your life is hidden with Christ in God." Colossians 3:1-3

Wow! The peace I felt gave me the strength and wisdom to pray for the perpetrators; that somehow they would come to know Jesus and not be in a position where they needed to steal from another ever again. I hoped that they would see the scriptures I had written that were in my purse and I prayed that they would have an encounter with Jesus.

Would they?

Would they see who I was because of the contents of my handbag?

Would they see Jesus in me?

A couple of days later, I was walking down a corridor at the gym and a lady walked by me. After she had gone past, I felt the need to turn around and unbelievably, as I did, so did she! We were now about 3 metres away from each other. I had never seen this woman before in my life.

She simply said to me, "You have Jesus in you. I felt it!"

Can you imagine?! Instantly, I smiled and said in a bewildered way, "I do! Yes! I do have Jesus in me!" I was almost expecting her to say, "So do I," but she just replied, "Can I hug you?" And she got hold of me and held me really tightly.

Again, she said, "You are full of Jesus," and then she carried on back down the corridor and I was standing there, probably looking slightly dumbstruck.

You see, I know Jesus is in me; He saved me, and He is my all, but it struck me that I had only been having that conversation with God a couple of days before. I was wondering if the handbag thieves would see Jesus. And God Himself showed me that no matter where you are or who you encounter, if Jesus is to be seen, it will happen!

I am a real woman and if you're reading this, you are a real person too!

But the best way I can Ellie'vate you today is to remind you of this.

JESUS IS REAL and our identity is in HIM!

Read ~ Colossians 3:3, Romans 6:6, 2 Thessalonians 2:14

Ellie'vation ~ If possible, try to find out more about your ancestry, about your parents, their parents, and even further back. Knowing where we come from, geographically, as well as spiritually, gives us a sense of who we are, and you may discover things that can blow your mind! I did!

Day 4

Do you feel excited? Do you feel prepared?

When I remember that God sees all and knows all, I feel excited! I know that He has such an incredible plan for my life. Do you realise that everything you've been through and everything that's going to happen, God already knows? That's why He prepares us. It's a beautiful story, a bestseller, waiting to unfold!

Maybe you're feeling hopeless, wretched, and daunted because of the state of the world, both naturally and politically, or perhaps situations are making you unhappy in your own immediate sphere, but today I want to Ellie'vate your mood by reminding you that your heart can be restored and revived! I want to remind you that there is a plan for you and a purpose and a reason for you being here! The fact that you are reading this right now, the fact that you woke up today, means there is MORE for you on this earth. More for you to do, and more areas for you to be efficient and productive in your service for God. You have things to do, people to meet, places to go, and blessings to receive! How exciting is that?!

If you are feeling exhausted, drained, and hopeless, I absolutely get it. I have been there before many times, and I know you will be thinking it won't ever change. But I promise you it will change. There comes a time when the weariness, the test, the draining, the wilderness season, ENDS! It is finished! And a new season begins. Hallelujah!

You realise that everything, every hurt, every loss, every wound, every sickness, every rejection, every sorrow, every shock, GOD WILL USE. He won't waste a thing. He's in the recycling business you know. Not one day in your life is misplaced. It's all part of his intricate plan. It's all part of your story.

Knowing that even my biggest blunders and ginormous gaffes are weaved into the dazzling, magnificent tapestry of my life story allows me to accept that the times I have cried rivers, well, they may just have watered down the murkiness of some

of my most distressing memories.

Knowing that our Father sees all and knows all stirs up the everlasting hope that I first learned about over two decades ago when I discovered Him……or should I say, when He said, "It is time."

So, get excited, get prepared today for whatever is coming! Because today you are alive! And you are alive in Him! Watch the plot thicken!

"For the vision is yet for the appointed time; it hastens toward the goal, and it will not fail. Though it tarries, wait for it; for it will certainly come, it will not delay" Habakkuk 2:3

If you feel you've messed up so much that there's no going back, don't believe it!

If you feel others have messed up things for you and there's no going back, don't believe it!

If you feel like God doesn't listen to any of your prayers, don't believe it!

If you feel like you're in the wrong place, don't believe it!

If you feel like you've blown your destiny, DO NOT EVER BELIEVE THAT!

There's a foundational plot to this story of yours; a prologue; a beginning. It may feel like your beginning has beginning has lasted 50 plus years! It has!

But God has an action packed, God ordained, highly blessed chapter coming up for you……….! You just have to turn the page and delve in!

Do you honestly think THIS IS IT? Do you literally believe that there isn't more to your story?

There is a lot more to your story and the 'plot truly does thicken!'

But there are steps to take……..

Step into the next chapter, written by the Almighty Father God by being obedient, by your offerings of praise and worship and by reading and listening to His Word.

God isn't a complex being! He is unbelievably simple. It's we humans who make things tangled, tortuous, and tough on ourselves. We consistently add unnecessary paragraphs into our stories……….too many garbled sentences……..we don't take a rest and reflect on our latest written words……….we just march right on……….looking in the wrong direction……….forcing ourselves into an entirely different plot, that was never meant to be part of the finished manuscript anyway!

So, today, to Ellie'vate your whole being, lay it all before Him; put down YOUR pen and let God put the finishing touches, the edits, to this next chapter. You haven't messed up. And God, being the Almighty Creator He is, can only ever produce a bestselling masterpiece.

That's you.

Read ~ Titus 3:5, 1 John 5:11, 1 Corinthians 15:1-4

Ellie'vate ~ Write down 3 sentences of your testimony. Do 3 more sentences tomorrow. Do this every day. In a year you'll have a book. You can share your God given testimony with the world!

Day 5

Now, where did I put those hiking boots?

'The pull of the mountain, is like gravity for my soul' (Heather Day Gilbert)

I'm not a flatlands kind of girl..........I'm not inspired by wandering around an expanse of 'sameness', existing on a plateau of assurance, safety, and sanctuary. Spiritually, My Lord has already confirmed my sanctuary in Him. It's written. It's a sealed deal!

But while I'm here on earth, I have so, so much to do! As a vessel for my Father in Heaven, there are so, so many souls to be saved! I haven't got the time or the disposition to be wandering around where it's safe, in the flatlands.........Because MY soul is saved! Granted, it's nice to take a rest and recently I have been MORE than commanded by my Father to rest! "Rest in Me, Ellie," said He.

No one knows more than the Lord what is coming next! He knows YOU! And He knows ME!

He knows I'm a mountain climber. But I'm not sauntering along the easy path, gradually making my way up the tourist route. You know; the classic, ready-made path with the odd tiny stone that might get stuck in your shoe. Kind of niggles at you, but you take off your shoe, shake it out and carry on meandering up the easy path.

No! I'm marching up the tougher terrain. There are always two ways to ascend a mountain. Any climber or fell runner knows that………and there are two ways down also! (This is not the time for me to tell of the day I was on a very steep fell run, came across a bull and didn't run back down……. No! I actually flew! For real……..but that's another story.)

Here, we're talking about getting up, not coming back down!

I'm looking up at this beautiful mountain in front of me called GROWTH. Mount Growth! I'm evaluating the climb, my technique, my navigational skills…………. and the strength and tenacity I am going to have to gather to reach the summit. It's here where you discover that your strength comes from the Lord. In the flatlands, you find happy, chilled out individuals who don't feel an inherent need to lean on the

 Lord. They have no need because they like where they are. It's comfortable and is maybe a time of blessing and relaxation; a time of contemplation and reflection on where they have been and where they are now.

But none of us should hang around there for too long. The journey doesn't end the minute all your so-called dreams come true and many of your desires have been fulfilled!

It's here, in the flatlands, where you should be praying and preparing for the next climb. You should be looking for your mountain!

When I saw Mount Growth, I prayed. I asked for wisdom to help me on the climb. I prayed about the parts of the mountain I couldn't see. I said, "Father God, My precious Father, in whom I trust, please give me revelation."

It was then I saw the crevices; I saw the jagged rocks that could cut me acutely; I saw possible splits in the path I had ascertained was the one I should take; dark areas that looked like an abyss; I couldn't quite see everything clearly because when you look far up the highest of mountains, there is a blinding mist. However, I knew as part of climbing Mount Growth, that it was at these crosswalks where I would have to press in more; that the Lord would be my eyes, my ears, and my guide.

Ellie'vation comes from allowing God to be your guide. Allowing Him to help you climb your mountain of growth.

> **"I press toward the goal for the prize of the upward call of God in Christ Jesus."** Philippians 3:14

When you are working for the Kingdom, the Lord's Kingdom, you WILL have mountains to climb. And even though it can be the toughest of times, you should also be praising Him. Praise Him for being with you every step of the way! Praise

Him for the growth. Praise Him because you truly are *that*

important to Him. God wants to take you to the next level. Are you ready? Have you prayed? Do you want to be a warrior in the Kingdom and fight with the Lord's army?

I do!

And as I commit to that journey and I look up, I start to notice on the path I have chosen to take, little grassy areas, situated here and there; actually many of them soft and safe on the climb, on the tough terrain where I can sit comfortably and wait on the Lord for His next instruction. It's whilst I'm sitting there that the mountain actually doesn't seem so huge now. I can see the summit. Usually, as we climb we sense the summit becoming further and further away....................but no!

I see the peaks, covered in snow, glistening, beckoning, "Ellie, come on, it's beautiful up here. And wait until you see what's on the other side!"

"She is not afraid of snow for her household, for all her household is clothed with scarlet." Proverbs 31:21

The Blood of Christ covers me and mine as we climb to the summit.

And then, I see Him...... His smile...... His arms outstretched...... My beautiful Lord......waiting. And I see the snowy peaks. They are glistening.........in the bright, intense, luminous Son, in the light of THE Son.

Now, where did I put those hiking boots? Prepare your footwear, and let's climb.

Let's Ellie'vate!

Read ~ Hebrews 6:1, Luke 8:14-15, Colossians 1:9-10

Ellie'vation ~ One of the best ways to Ellie'vate is to move, so today take a walk in nature somewhere brand new. Breathe in fresh air and marvel at the beauty of God's world. Ask God to show you something new and to speak to you in new ways.

Day 6

Not Every Table is God's Table

There are some tables I have been invited to sit at with some groups of people and I am happy to join them. There are some tables that I haven't wanted to eat at and I'm glad I haven't been invited. However, there have been a couple of tables over the last 20 years that I thought I really wanted to sit at and break bread with the other diners. But I wasn't invited. And that made me sad. Years later I would discover exactly why God hadn't allowed me to sit and break bread with those particular people.

And that made me relieved and thankful.

At times we don't understand God's rationale and He doesn't make things clear to us instantly, but I know that a little flash of Ellie'vation can go a long way!

So read on!

God won't give you a seat at specific tables because they're unfortunately the sort of tables that Jesus would be chucking over if He were walking amongst us right now! These groups and cliques and particular ministries believe that they don't want you involved with them, but sincerely, God will move heaven and earth to make sure you aren't caught up with the wrong crowd!

It is God who doesn't want YOU at THEIR table!

I have noticed a shift in the way some people reach out to God and it's unnerving. They chase conferences, celebrity leaders, supernatural movements, and slick, beautifully marketed churches, but they don't seem to want to chase God, in their own living room. I chat with people sometimes and they look at me like I'm strange if I ask about their latest encounter with the Holy Spirit on their own, in their own home, in prayer. A new, growing, generation of Christians are being taught that they'll only tap into the Holy Spirit at the rise of a certain beat in a tune, and that "Amen" is said after every sentence a celebrity preacher utters. Even a sentence such as," And my Lamborghini was sprayed in the shade I decided, AMEN??"

The only 'supernatural' we should ever be chasing is our supernatural God. He is all powerful, all consuming, and Almighty. No human on earth can substitute for God. It's important to reflect on what exactly we are looking for when we yearn for a 'place at the table.'

Are you looking for fulfilment? That comes from God.

Are you looking for love? That comes from God.

Are you looking to be recognised? God sees you.

Are you looking for nourishment? God has all the nourishment you need in His word.

The seats, the doors, the rooms, the towns, the countries where God wants you to be will all be clear invitations to you.

And you won't be rejected or replaced by anyone.

Chase God, not people, and watch what our mighty Lord does.

You'll be Ellie'vated to heights you didn't even know existed!

Read ~ Psalm 23:5, Isaiah 21:5, Psalm 78:19

Ellie'vation ~ Think about the people you know and write down who you would love to prepare a formal dinner for. It has to be a network of people who don't know each other and no more and no less than six people. Now plan it!

Day 7

Look at what can happen!

Abraham and his story in Genesis never

fail to remind me what can happen if we just have a deep, unmoving faith in God and faith in how He wants to use us and bless us. Not only did Abraham have a great faith, but additionally his obedience was exponential! He was in, what seemed, a hopeless situation! God had asked him to sacrifice his own precious son, Isaac. And he was even willing to do this because God told him to. I want that kind of faith! He literally trusted God's goodness so much that even when he was asked to do the worst thing imaginable, to murder his own son, his faith was such that he knew he could leave it to God. He knew that he could trust God and that His plan was to bless Abraham, not to hurt or harm him. Wow!

Well, we know that now. But what was Abraham really thinking as he was walking up the mountain with Isaac travelling alongside him? I am in awe at his strength of character and his focus on doing precisely what God had asked of him! If that had been me, I would have more than likely told my daughter about God's plan and that she and I needed to come up with a plan to appease Him!! I'm just being honest!

However, so that you and I had the choice to live eternally with Him in heaven, God *did* sacrifice His only Son.

He did that freely, for our freedom.

And so, I continue to pray for a faith as deep, as trusting, as strength-filled and as obedient as Abraham's faith.

Perhaps you are facing unthinkable circumstances today. Perhaps you need more than a little Ellie'vation. But sometimes, just one tiny lift can help you take another step and another step, and one more step, and one more step, and that's all it takes to keep going. To keep moving up the mountain to where your Father God awaits.

Stay resolute in your belief that God WILL come through for you. Stay in faith. Obey His Word.

He is the same God.

Read ~ Romans 1:12, Romans 15:13, Hebrews 11:3

Ellie'vate ~ Get a jar. Get some paper. Write down all the things you want to do that need really strong, deep faith in God to be achieved. Write the date on each one and cut, fold, and put in the jar. Pray and believe. Have faith! Every time you achieve one thing take it out of the jar. One day the jar will be empty.

Day 8

Encourage yourself!

Sometimes I say to myself, "You are dripping in FAVOUR!"

I have come to learn that the best mornings to declare this is when I'm dealing with onslaught. Opposition of all kinds!

It's fair to say that the last seven years of my life I have been on a journey of severe and substantial physical health issues that at times I thought were never going to ease.

Yet also during this season, because it has been a specific season, I have been drenched in the favour of God!

It probably won't look like that to some people, but to the favoured ones that have stood by my side through this period, who understand the power of favour and the responsibility and the warfare that comes with the favour of God, it has been all too clear to see.

It's only in hindsight that we can ever say, "I wouldn't change a thing." However, as I sit here today, with excruciating pain in my neck and back, I do yearn to be pain-free. But would I have had the revelation, the intimacy, the desperate moments of grief, the cleansing, the stripping of self and ego, if I had sailed through the last seven years without a single obstacle? I believe not.

What is Ellie'vation? It's me, Ellie, wanting to share with you some tiny epiphany I dared to embrace in my moments of strain. Moments when God gave me glimpses of the gold to be bestowed and the woman to be shaped when she exited the refiner's fire.

If that's not the favour of God, to be refined in His fire, what is?

The process of refining gold requires a craftsman to sit next to a scorching hot fire with smelted, liquefied gold in a huge melting pot and he must keep stirring the liquid and separate the impurities and sediment that continues to rise to the top of the pot.

To rise higher in our walk with God, to Ellie'vate in life in general, is so much easier if we

aren't carrying heavy burdens. That's why being refined, allowing God to bring all our impurities to the surface, our sin, our pain, our darkest moments, is the surest way to grow and be set free to be all that you can be!

When you pray for favour, ask for the favour that causes opposition. Ask for the favour that petrifies the enemy! Ask for the favour that makes a difference to your soul, not just your bank account.

Do you trust Him with your whole life enough to ask Him for that favour?

Favour doesn't look like we always think it should look! It isn't owning a big, fancy house or a flash sports car. It isn't wearing designer clothes. Yes, God can pour out favour upon you financially and you may choose those things. But I believe the real favour of God is when He, the great Master Craftsman, has His eyes constantly upon you, stirring and stirring, collecting the impurities, and waiting until the gold is ready.

Until He can see His image in that gold.

Dripping in gold has a whole new meaning now, doesn't it?

Dripping in gold, dripping in FAVOUR.

Read ~ Proverbs 3:4, 2 Corinthians 6:2, Psalm 90:17

Ellie'vation ~ Invite the Holy

Spirit to show you where you need favour. He is waiting for you to welcome Him into your day. I can guarantee He will show you exactly what to pray for and it might just be something you hadn't even thought of!

Day 9

There's no need to see beyond the bend

I know you can't see what's around the corner.

Neither can I. Neither can they. But I DO know Who can.

Ahead of you and I is the vastness of the future. The great unknown. Nobody in the whole world has ever been there. It's a physically unvisited place but it feels like we've swung by there a thousand times.

However, it isn't unfamiliar to our God.

You see, God is permanently unchangeable. He is unceasing, everlasting, and eternal.

He is already there in our future. He isn't worried about what might happen. He isn't panicking and wishing, and assuming what could go right, what could go wrong.

He is there.

And this will Ellie'vate you right now!

Because He is already there, in your future, and not a thing can catch Him off guard, or make him jump, or surprise Him, He *knows* every single thing that is going to happen in your life! And do you know there are an absolute ton of promises in the Bible regarding your future? Yes, there are! Take a look! They are good promises.

He promises that He will never leave you. Amen!

He promises to pour out His compassion on you. Amen!

He promises His love will endure FOREVER. Amen!

He promises good and perfect gifts. Amen!

He promises to refresh your soul. Amen!

He promises to withhold no good thing from those whose walk is blameless. Amen!

He promises to be a refuge in times of trouble. Amen!

He promises to care for those who trust Him. Amen!

He promises to be with us when times are hard. Amen!

He promises to give us a future of hope. Amen!

He promises us His peace to guard our hearts and our minds. Amen!

He promises us eternal life. Amen!

You can relax knowing your future is in good hands. Your eternal future is in good hands. It's in God hands. If that's your will.

Make sure you let Him know and I can promise you in complete faith your future's so bright you're going to need shades!

Read ~ 2 Corinthians 4:17-18, Lamentations 3:21-23, Proverbs 16:1-4

Ellie'vation ~ Write a letter to the future you with all your current thoughts, feelings, what is happening in your life, what you're looking forward to, what things you want to change, what goals you have, then put it away somewhere safe and don't open it until 5 years from today. You'll be amazed at how much WILL have changed!

Day 10

Walk down this new path

Every single sentence written in the

Bible is there because God wanted it there. There isn't one chapter or scripture put in there by mistake. It tells us in 2 Timothy 3:16, **"All scripture is given by inspiration of God, and is profitable for doctrine, for reproof, for correction, and for instruction in righteousness…."**

One scripture that has been highlighted to me over the last few years is, **"And do not be conformed to this world, but be transformed by the renewing of your mind, that you may prove what is that good and acceptable and perfect will of God."** Romans 12:2

In 2017, I was involved in an accident that left me with injuries that I still live with today. I suffered a traumatic brain injury and whilst I won't go into that here (this devotional is about Ellie'vating you!) I do want to share something that helped me discover an incredible tool!

The scripture, Romans 12:2, kept jumping out at me. No matter what I read, whether my Bible or a devotional, or if a friend sent me an encouraging text message, or maybe I was listening to a sermon on YouTube, this scripture would keep presenting itself to me. Daily!

I realised God was trying to tell me something!

So, I studied it in depth. And I also decided to study the mind in depth, and whilst I was at it, I studied the brain in depth too! Now, let's not lose the irony in this. I was suffering badly with my injury. I couldn't even read for most days of the week. I struggled to look at a computer. The pain in my head was constantly immense. Consequently, I relied on my daughter to help me a lot.

On top of this, I had other injuries too that left me in a great deal of constant pain.
But I just knew in my heart I was going to discern something GOOD if I could just RENEW MY MIND! Because God said it!

And I was so determined I cried. I cried through the pain. I cried because I didn't understand.

I cried because I didn't like the path I was on, and I cried because I was hugely frustrated. Oh, and I cried because when I cried the crying made my head hurt even more!

Quite a lot of tears really, eh?

'You number my wanderings; Put my tears in your bottle; Are they not in your book?" Psalm 56:8

And so, I discovered that when you have suffered a traumatic brain injury, one of the most formidable long-term consequences can be an increased risk of dementia. Certainly, dismayed to read about this, especially after already discovering that my energy management was tantamount to preventing blackouts, I realised that God had already known all of this and because He had told me I was going to discern something GOOD if I could just RENEW MY MIND, well, I wasn't going to focus on this awful information and I was going to continue researching my renewal!

It was then I discovered neuroplasticity.

Gosh, God is mind blowing! I mean, WOW! He made our bodies, our brains, our minds, and I cannot fathom the detail He put into us. I say mind blowing because He literally does that to me every day! He BLOWS MY MIND!

When God fashioned our organ called the brain, He designed it in a way that after injury, whether minor or major, it was, well, almost irrepressible. But it would need help. And that's where we come in! So always make sure you are **'not destroyed through lack of knowledge!'** Hosea 4:6

Neuroplasticity introduces us to our need to discover new things, acquire fresh knowledge and master unfamiliar proficiencies. The brain creates brand new neural pathways with every fresh, new action you begin, so for example, you decide to learn the Japanese language, you start a Flamenco

dance class, you walk a new route to the shops, you try eating something you haven't eaten before; literally absolutely anything that is something new to you produces a new neural pathway in your brain.

Where I had suffered damage, it affected how I spoke and sometimes even now if my brain becomes extremely exhausted, I will speak 'gobbledygook'. Also, I would forget why I was doing something, and those areas stay damaged, but my brain has now produced new neural pathways and has even transferred functions that were in the damaged parts of my brain over to healthy parts.

It's like taking a detour! But it's a good detour! And that's what neuroplasticity does.

Consequently, creating new neural pathways can be a step forward in the prevention of dementia.

To Ellie'vate you today can I suggest that you do something completely unfamiliar, a change from normality for you. Try not to rely on routine so much or plan a day when you can do this. Who knows where this might lead?

God knows what He's doing!

He ALWAYS knows what He's doing.

Read ~ 2 Corinthians 4:16, John 8:32, Isaiah 40:31

Ellie'vation ~ Even though as humans we love to establish routines, try doing something out of routine today. Your brain will be thankful! Pick a new topic that the whole family can learn about or order a book on a subject you know nothing about. Follow and cook a brand new recipe or eat food you've never tasted before. This will Ellie'vate your brain structure!

Day 11

Get back up!

A few years ago, I had a spine surgery, quite a major one and only a short time after, I sensed God was telling me to, "Get back up". At the time, I couldn't understand, because I wasn't able to walk properly and was also wearing a brace for support and because I couldn't hold myself up and straight without it. I was due to speak at a ladies' conference within a couple of months, so I thought to myself, 'Wow, God wants me ready!' I honestly thought He meant I was to just start walking and moving but this was proving impossible. I was in a lot of pain and plenty of healing was needed. I certainly couldn't just 'get back up!' It was a tough time for me because I am a very independent person and if I need to ask for help, I struggle to do this. It was during this painful time that I kept getting that phrase in all sorts of ways! 'Get back up!' Whether this was in prayer, or I heard something on the TV, or somebody said something to me!

Suddenly, one day, the phrase made sense. 'Get back-up!' I understood immediately. I needed help, physically and emotionally.

And God was telling me to get some physical and emotional back-up!

He wanted me to reach out to others and let people know that I was struggling! I was so private and ridiculously independent, that I didn't even allow people to visit me in the hospital for 3 weeks after the surgery! And God was telling me, "Go and let people know you need help. Get back-up!"

Over the next couple of days, why not contact a couple of friends and ask them to agree with you in prayer? Send the scriptures and prayers that you will be praying at home and ask them to declare and decree the truth and promises of God's Word over you when they are in their own prayer time, and you can do the same for them.

None of us feel as Ellie'vated and full of joy than when our friends lift us up in prayer and when we know our friends and family have got our back.

So be Ellie'vated today by making sure you 'get back-up!'

Read ~ Ecclesiastes 4:9-12, Galatians 6:2, Hebrews 10:24-25

Ellie'vation ~ Each one of us has strengths and if we share our strengths with others that's what makes the dream come true! Teamwork makes the dream work! Today, make sure your church, your community, knows about your strengths so you can be called upon when someone is in need.

Day 12

Why did it take so long?

Why did it take so long for me to realise that free will won't necessarily lead to freedom!

I asked God that very question this morning.............

It was when I realised that these days, even in the midst of huge concerns, dramatic changes, and unknown steps about to be taken; I know that I know that I know, the Lord is in control!

And acknowledging that is the best feeling in the world!

The reason He is in control is because……. I asked Him to be! You see, we are accorded free will. And that's cool but I don't particularly think it's the way to conduct our lives all the time. And in the past, yikes, the free will decisions I have made caused me nothing but the opposite of freedom! I've felt trapped, imprisoned, and desperate to escape! That's not freedom! Just free will!

Granted, I love to choose which dessert I am about to eat.

But when it comes to the important things in life, for example,

which crucial steps to take or when some life changing choices have arisen and I'm wondering which is the most fruitful path to take, I really do love to leave it all up to Him, prayerfully considering my options. But it wasn't always like that.

It's in prayer and meditation that He will advise, lead and counsel. We cannot expect to instantly know which steps to take or even if the Lord wants us to stay quite still for a while. We have to spend time with Him and pray to Him and through the Spirit.

But I can guarantee that the freedom you feel when literally allowing God free rein over your

life is of the utmost comfort! In fact, words really cannot describe it so I can only suggest you try it! It's a case of being obedient to His will and not trying to control a situation by leaning on your own understanding…….. remember the scripture?

"And so find favour and high esteem in the sight of God and man. Trust in the LORD with all your heart and lean not on your own understanding. In all your ways acknowledge Him, and He shall direct your paths." Proverbs 3:4,5,6

So, for me, why did it take so long to give up the reins??

Because………. (I'm standing up now), "My name is Ellie Palma-Cass, and I used to be a control freak."

For years, I was a control freak. To be honest, I don't think I was a 'freak' per se, whatever that means?! But I did try to control everything. It was in order to prevent hurt, pain, and disorganisation in my existence. Oh, I had the control freak thing bad!

And, unfortunately, it continued for years into my life as a Christian too. Healing can come in an instant for some or over many years of pressing into the Lord for a breakthrough for others. It took some time for me.

But, when you believe in God and His healing power, whether for emotional or physical sickness, it will manifest! When the timing is right. Not our timing! His timing!

There will come a period in your life when you know that the best way forward is to say, "Not my will Lord, but Yours."

And there is no better way to Ellie'vate! That is Ellie'vation right there!

Now, I did used to pray like that but then my prayers would continue with, "But please can……..," and all the following words would be the opposite to my giving Him control! It was actually pointless for me to even bother the Lord with, "Not my will, Lord, but Yours," as I didn't mean it! I thought I did! But I didn't!

However, after many, many years of being a Christian woman, I have finally and, I have to say, happily, given God the reins!

It was a long time coming but it's worth it. Now, I may not like something that's happening in my life; an issue I have to

contend with; a situation arising that I want to react to; an injustice, or even a dream that doesn't seem to be materialising……..

But you know what? It's not my issue, my injustice, or my problem! Because God told me to give it all to Him and He'll deal with it, and He does! I'm not suggesting any of us don't step out in faith here, or that we should sit back and let the world go by. I'm just offering a little advice, a little wisdom maybe, a massive dose of Ellie'vation hopefully!

Fundamentally, when you've done all you can do, it's time to step back and let God set in motion His perfect plan!

And it's precisely because He is in control!

We are human, and we can all have good and bad days; we can act or react; we can make a mistake and we can kick ourselves; we can choose to believe and trust, or not believe and not trust but when you allow God to take control and press into Him and all that He stands for I can assure you, with a huge smile on my face, that for you, it might not need to take so long!

Give God every part of your life and every part of your life will be God! (filled!)

Is there any other way you would want to live?

If you're going through something today; if you feel you need an answer but it's not materialising; if you need God to act on your behalf; then get down on your knees, thank Him for being the God of your life, and relinquish control. Hold on loosely.

Then watch what He does.

Read ~ Galatians 5:13, Joshua 24:15, 1 Corinthians 10:13

Ellie'vation ~ Listen to the song Whatever Your Plan Is - Sung by Josie Buchanan - Bethel Music.

Day 13

It's never too late!

One of the most encouraging comments I have ever received was at a conference where I was speaking when I chatted with a lady after the meeting. This lady said to me that she had really enjoyed my testimony and that I had encouraged her. She said, "You've made me excited for the future!" Do you know, this lady was 92 years old! Can you imagine how encouraged I felt at hearing that? You are never too old – it's never too late – and I firmly believe that if you need to receive a second wind at life, if you pray and believe, it will come!

The day you were born, you arrived slap, bang, and wallop into this *natural* realm to make an impact for the *supernatural* realm! Your potential is there EVERY day, so use it! Chase it! Anything can happen!

Imagine the honour of being 92 years old and God still has work for you to do on His earth? Wow! What a privilege! I love to spend time with anyone who is over the age of 80. They just seem to have so much to say yet it can be said in one sentence! Have you ever noticed that? A Godly gent or lady in their later years is a blessing in your life and you can also be a blessing to them!

The fact that the lady who spoke to me at the meeting was so excited about the future, even thought she was 92 years old, doesn't surprise me too much. Firstly, she was a Christian. She knew that God was with her and that He can use us at any given time and on any given day; we just have to be ready and willing. He is no respecter of persons. If He wishes to use a 92 year old woman to change the hearts of a village, He will.

Moses was 80 years old when he first began his real, God-given mission work. 80! God appointed him to be the man who escorted the Jews from their captivity in Egypt. This was a huge commission and Moses was chosen to be their leader, guide, mentor, encourager, intercessor, navigator, you name it! His burden was heavy, and he was an old man! Yet God had plans for him, and you might say these were the BEST years of his life! He was making a huge impact. Age didn't stop him, and it absolutely didn't stop God from using him!

I have a friend Janine, who has done more frontline mission work in her late 50's and early 60's than ever in her younger years. And God-willing, that's her plan for the rest of her life. She will continue to serve God, preaching and reaching and teaching needy, desperate children in Kenya until well past her 80's! I know this for a fact. You see, God knows she wants to make an impact in the *natural* realm for the *supernatural* realm and age won't stop her!

Some of the most well-known preachers and revivalists conducted much of their work in later life. John Wesley, George Muller and the two ladies who kindled with prayer the Outer Hebridean revival, were all effective and engaged well into their 80's.

Old age is the favour of God. It's not a mistake that you are still here. Use the prudence, foresight, knowledge, and wisdom that God has bestowed upon you to bless the ones the Lord places in your path. If you don't see them, pray for them to come!

Be Ellie'vated today! It's never too late! **"They will still yield fruit in old age; they shall be full of sap and very green."** Psalm 90:9 (ESV)

Read ~ Proverbs 16:16, Ephesians 5:15-16, Proverbs 19:8

Ellie'vation ~ See if you can set up an older/younger mentor prayer partner team in your church or community.

Day 14

Pursue those goals

When I became a Christian over 20

years ago, I remember people talking about 'the prayer of Jabez'. I thought Jabez was somebody in the church and I wondered what he prayed that was so exciting! Did he have some extra connection to God? Was he praying in a certain way? What did he receive because of this specific prayer he prayed? It was all strangely mysterious to me! And to be honest, I couldn't wait to meet him!

One day a lady at that church gifted me with a little hard back book and guess what it was called? Yes! The Prayer of Jabez!

Jabez was in the Bible! Not in my church!

In the first year of my newly found, thriving faith and flourishing relationship with Jesus, I didn't read the Old Testament. I read the New Testament, so I hadn't heard of Jabez. I absolutely love reading the Old Testament now, well, I love every single sentence of the Bible! I've been reading it for all of 20 years and it still amazes me that I learn something new all the time. That's because the Word of God is alive! I say to people frequently, "I could eat it because I love it so much!" and that's the truth!

The words that Jabez spoke to the God of Israel were,

"Oh, that you would bless me and enlarge my territory!

Let your hand be with me, and keep me from harm

So that I will be free from pain."

And then it is written that God 'granted his request.'

We read about Jabez ever so briefly in 1 Chronicles, but one of my favourite Old Testament books is Jeremiah and it's in this book that we will receive some magnificent Ellie'vation today!

Through His Word, God emboldens us to persevere and persist when it comes to pursuing our goals and aims in life. He wants us to accomplish great things and triumph in our missions! He shows us this in many places and through many lives throughout the Bible, and in the book of Jeremiah, He tells us that there is a plan and a purpose for each one of us. A plan of prosperity, happiness, victory, achievement, elation, and delight!

From time to time, I hear people say they don't think God has a plan for them, or they feel they've missed the plan God had for them. Or they feel too old and it's too late for the plan. None of these statements are true!

God's plan for you is implanted right in your heart! He has thus far placed in you an inclination to accomplish and demonstrate His work on earth.

If you're wondering to yourself what that plan is, then the most strategic thing you can do is pray!

Another of my 'own' scriptures is in Jeremiah too! I call them my 'own' because they're such significant scriptures in my life. They are the scriptures that I have clung on to and have prayed, declared, and decreed and God has always responded! Jeremiah 33.3, "Call to me and I will tell you things you don't know…………"

God is telling you if you don't know what the plan is, call to Him and He will tell you! You ought to listen!

Before we bring Jabez in, let me share a couple of things that may help you to hear from God and discover your plan!

I believe your passions hold some clue to God's plans for you. If you love to sing and have a wonderful voice, you could produce an album of songs for worship and the words could change the worship experience of thousands. If you love to write, you may write articles or books that make the readers happy or lead them to know the Lord. You could be a fantastic rugby player and love playing for your team and it could open doors for people to know the Lord. The opportunities are endless! So, look at your passions and what you adore spending time pursuing.

Another way of looking at this is to ask yourself, if you didn't have to weigh up money restrictions or time restrictions, what would you really spend your days doing? What do you feel is the deepest desire of your heart?

I know that you know.

Because when we pray and we are completely honest with ourselves and with God, when we're in that still, silent, contemplative place with our Father, we already know the innermost yearnings of our soul.

Perhaps it's time to be brave. The key is to have confidence in God, have faith in God and let Him know it's all systems go!

That's what I did and here's how I did it with my Jabez prayer. And God has never stopped blowing my mind!

Primarily, Jabez prayed, "BLESS me and ENLARGE MY TERRITORY." In the same way I use the Lord's prayer as an example as is suggested, I use this prayer as an example, and I tailor it and so can you. You might ask God to bless you with insight, understanding, discernment and opportunities. Pray for Him to bless your household and business with financial provision and wisdom to make good decisions.

After that, Jabez appealed of the Lord, "Let YOUR HAND be WITH ME." You could ask God to pour out His spirit upon you, counsel you, and give you peace, patience, and forgiveness. Ask God to help your thoughts be His thoughts.

Finally, Jabez said, "Keep me FROM HARM so that I will be FREE FROM PAIN." Pray for God's protection and that He

surrounds you with His mightiest of warrior angels. Declare and decree God's promise to you that no weapon formed against you will prosper and that every tongue that rises up against you in judgement you shall condemn. Ask God to protect you from any plans of evil. Pray these prayers for you, your loved ones, your animals, your businesses, too.

Remember, after Jabez had cried out to the Lord, it is written that God granted His request. I believe God will say YES and AMEN to your prayer too. He certainly did and still does to my prayers!

So be Ellie'vated today!

When you recognise God's plan is your plan and it's already in your heart, you can make a decision today to pray, set things in motion, and pursue those goals!

Read ~ James 1:17, 1 Corinthians 2:9, James 1:12

Ellie'vate ~ Grow something from seed. Maybe you're already a super gardener but if you're not, decide to nurture a plant from the very beginning. Or grow herbs in your kitchen. It's so much fun to watch things grow that you've planted.

Day 15

Anything can happen!

Today as you slipped out of bed, popped on your gown, wafted down to the kitchen, and popped the kettle on, ready for your first cuppa, did you think "Yippee! A new day! I have a few things on my mind, a few situations need dealing with head on, a couple of concerns need resolving but with God behind me I can DO ALL THINGS through Him who strengthens me!"

Or, as you sipped your hot drink, did you think, "Oh no, another day. I have to go into work, and I can't stand working with that woman; the traffic is going to be on go-slow with all this rain. How am I going to make the dinner tonight as I need to shop and there's no time because I'm at that Bible study later……"?

I hope and I pray that it was the first scenario. You see, the minute you acknowledge and accept that God is right behind you, is the minute you are proving your belief in Him. And when you are faithful, He is eager to please!

Make up your mind that the second scenario isn't going to be. Select the correct thoughts and determine that you will not be defeated by negative thinking today!

To be Ellie'vated today, don't fill your mind with miserable thoughts no matter what is going on in your life. Because your strength WILL RISE as you declare positive and powerful decrees over your day. Thank Him for everything He is doing.

Do a study on all the scriptures in the Bible that speak of God's help. You'll be amazed at just how much He wants to be in every detail of your day. And remember, with a positive mindset and trust in the Lord today,

ANYTHING CAN HAPPEN!

Read ~ Isaiah 55:8-9, Isaiah 43:19, Psalm 90:14

Ellie'vation ~ Instead of emailing someone, why not write a letter or send a card? Receiving a card through the letterbox these days can be so unusual, yet it can Ellie'vate the mood of anyone! So, think of someone you know who would benefit from receiving a letter or card with an encouraging, warm message and write it today.

Day 16

Why, thank you!

Do you have a gratitude journal? I can't emphasise enough how important and life-changing it can be to list all the things you are grateful for in your life. Many years ago, when I was in a period of utter despondency and struggling to find anything to be thankful for at all, I sat on my bed in tears and noticed a torn piece of paper on my bedside table.

Even though I felt beaten down and couldn't see the priceless gift I had, my life, and I struggled to acknowledge the blessing that another day had been given to me, a sweeping thought popped into my head. "That lady I saw earlier smiled at me; the plumber has fixed my washer and fitted it correctly under the worktop; I saw a precious new-born duckling and my heart swelled; I can make a hot chocolate drink and enjoy it even more because there is fresh whipped cream in the fridge".

It hit me! I had to write down these little gifts in my day that I was grateful for. They seem like tiny, inconsequential things but they are mighty when we add them all up. Writing five things down every single day in an old, disused notebook I found in a drawer was one of the best things I could have done. It forced me to look for the good in my day and it helped me to begin getting stronger emotionally.

These days I use a gratitude journal and it is filled with no end of precious memories that I can look back on. And I treat myself to beautiful, large notebooks. Yes! I have pages and pages of gratitude and, as I look over the years of pages, I see that even though I didn't know it at the time, as I wrote something simple, yet beautiful down, within the next 24 hours the joy I felt would have an impact on somebody else.

It made me think about how so much of what we do can have a ripple effect. Whether that's a good effect or a bad one. One of the ways I choose to bless people is to encourage. I am a natural encourager. It makes me happy to do that and I suppose I am as blessed as the person being encouraged!

But going back to the ripple effect, we can choose whether we bless someone or hurt someone. When we hurt another, they could already be having a bad day, and who knows if our comment is the last straw, and they just give up.

When we make somebody happy, they may feel so incredibly exuberant that they then go on to do commit a huge loving gesture for someone else!

The ripple effect is powerful!

Moreover, I believe sowing and reaping is a powerful effect too! If truth be told, the ripple effect is borne from sowing and reaping. If you sow kindness, generosity, mercy, love, and graciousness into the lives of others, in due time you will reap the rewards. If you sow nasty gossip and wicked words, the same will be reaped by you.

To Ellie'vate your mood right now, pledge to only sow kindness, to only bless and not curse, and to be thankful for the tiniest, simplest things in your day.

Say, "Why, thank you!" to your Father in Heaven and watch the Lord make positive ripples all around you!

Read ~ Psalm 105:1, Isaiah 12:4-5, 1 Thessalonians 5: 16-18

Ellie'vation ~ Buy a beautiful book and decide to journal. If you already journal, create a new book with ephemera and design it to suit your style. Make a special box to keep all your journals safe and tidy.

Day 17

I've got the power!

You have the power! "Do I?" you're thinking. Yes, YOU have the power to change any situation in your day. It all comes down to what thoughts you allow and how long you let them stay. Now generally, we only ever really want to change our situation if it's a bad one, or if it's uncomfortable. But it's in the painful and tough circumstances where we grow. And where we allow ourselves to grow is where we get stronger, thus, we realise we have the power to change our situation and learn from it.

An intuitive way to view your circumstances is to look at them from a different perspective. Our perception and then the reality of a situation can be oceans apart, yet a swift perspective change can fuel your strength and change your focus. Whenever I get a fleeting bad thought in my mind or an image that I know isn't from God, I instantly put a big red X through it and declare this isn't real.

Did you know that a feeling can only last if the thought does? That's a fact! Ultimately, as soon as you change the thought to something positive, you change your mood to feeling positive! Now do you believe me when I say, "You've got the power?" If you continually hold on to a perspective, an outlook, which produces fear, you are in bondage. Enslaved to thoughts and fears that serve no part in Ellie'vation!

There is a story in the Bible about a woman who had 'a spirit of infirmity for eighteen years and was bent over and could in no way raise herself up.' Whenever I think of this woman I feel her pain because I remember the agony I was in before I had a spine surgery some years ago and I could not get up, walk, or even move on my own, without extreme pain. I know now it was because splinters of my spine were floating around in my blood and my lower spine was slowly disintegrating. Our spine is what holds us up. When it came time for an emergency surgery I was unable to move. The splinters were short of cutting my spinal cord and I was blessed to be saved from being paralysed. Hallelujah!

However, God showed me a different perspective! Many people are bent over, unable to raise themselves up because of the way they are thinking. Because their thought life isn't Christ-filled; isn't good and pure and lovely. When we are concentrating on anything that isn't Kingdom related it can cause us to become sick; heartsick. As Christians everything we do should revert back to our Lord and Saviour, Jesus. Is this what Jesus would think? Is this what Jesus would do? Is this what Jesus would say? Whenever I ask myself those questions it reminds me of what is important, of who I am, of Who I represent.

To Ellie'vate yourself today, try this. Whenever you get a momentary thought that threatens your peaceful momentum, put a big red X through it and declare this isn't real!

Stand tall. Keep your spine straight. Raise yourself up.

Remember! YOU have the power!

Read ~ Matthew 6:33, 2 Corinthians 5:7, 1 John 2:15-17

Ellie'vate ~ Remind yourself today of all the things your body has done for you and all it does. You may have produced children, run an Ironman, carried huge bags of shopping while pushing a pram, climbed mountains like Everest.....you may even save lives with your hands. Our bodies are incredible! Be thankful for every part of it and remember every part of it is important!

Day 18

None of us are perfect

If you mentally beat yourself up about the resentful feelings you may hold for someone let me share a story with you. I'm hoping it will stop you doing that but also realise that there's invariably a different perspective and a bigger picture.

I have a friend whose father was a solitary man, who rarely spoke. When she was growing up, he worked all hours and they seldom saw him. He was a good provider for the family. When he was at home, even though he wasn't a hostile man he never conveyed his pride in anything they achieved at school or in sports and dance clubs and he never told them he loved them.

As we all grew up and went our separate ways, we stayed in touch and my friend, who I will call Melissa, got married and had two little girls. She was happy. Unfortunately, her mother died at a relatively young age and Melissa struggled to stay in touch with her father. Nonetheless, when she discovered he had suffered a massive heart attack and was in hospital she wanted to bring him to live with her and her little family. He settled in with her and Melissa had help from a community care nurse. They were helping him to get dressed one day and

Melissa saw large scars across his back and shoulders, something she hadn't ever seen before. They were old scars. She was shocked, but she didn't want to bring up any unsettling memories for him, so she rang her uncle, her father's younger brother, to see if he knew anything about these injuries.

Melissa was devastated to hear that her dad had experienced agonising abuse at the hands of his father as a child, and most of the time his injuries were acquired as he protected his younger brothers and sisters from their father's wrath. Melissa was distraught and aghast. She didn't have a clue about his childhood, and she saw her dad in a whole new light. Furthermore, she understood how difficult her father must have found it to share his feelings and emotions with them, his own children, because he carried so much pain and rejection. She was determined to show him just how much he was loved and help him to get healing from God.

None of us can switch lives with anybody.

We can't reverse and revert to babyhood and demand a different set of parents. I'm sure it would be appealing to some of us, but it's a pointless thing to dwell on. However, when we find out about the background of our parents it can help us to understand them more, and that can lead to forgiveness. It certainly helped me to forgive two people in my biological family who had less than perfect childhoods, filled with absolute rejection.

Yet, we can also hold resentment because of the pain we have been caused by our parents. God knew that this would happen, but He still chose the parents we have. We can't understand everything God allows, but we can trust in His bigger picture. He knows the end from the beginning. And you can rest in the knowledge that God is holding on to you, holding on to you tight! He IS the perfect, unblemished, matchless, and faultless parent, and He wants you to know He will

never fail you or abandon you.

To Ellie'vate your whole being today, don't beat them up and don't beat yourself up! Fix your mind on Him. The One who, when your heart is overwhelmed with hurt, will comfort you forevermore.

Read ~ Romans 3:23, Romans 8:28, Psalm 71:20-24

Ellie'vation ~ Embrace the in-between. Today, decide not to fill spaces of time doing something for something's sake. Embrace the in-between times by just being. Breathe. Be still.

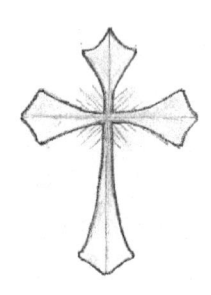

Day 19

Everybody hurts......sometimes

When something hurts, we call it a wound.

Many years ago, when I first became a woman of faith, I remember envisioning my heart. I saw it with a big, thick scar upon it and further, smaller scars surrounding the larger one. I had been steadily, emotionally wounded throughout my life, and I knew why I saw my heart that way. But as I healed, even though extremely slowly, I would think of that vision I had of my heart and I perceived the scars weren't reducing in size, but they were fading. The scars were there, but the scar tissue wasn't as prominent.

I can still feel my physical scars. They protrude from my skin. I don't mind. They remind me of how mighty God is and the circumstances I have overcome. I reminisce on the healing power of my Father in heaven. I have a scar across the top of my back acquired some years ago from a large tumour removal in the week before my 40th birthday. At the time I called it my tumour of pain. I felt as if all the grief and betrayal I had suffered at the loss, to me, of my son, was wrapped up in that tumour. Anger, resentment, bitterness, rage, shock, utter, utter devastation at the treachery and deception, at what one human can do to another………. I was ravaged. I was ruined. I was demolished in my heart.

That tumour was removed, and I swiftly healed emotionally.

I touch the scar at the base of my spine and the scars on my arm and my wrist and my head. Major emergency spine surgery that prevented me from being paralysed. An almost fatal road accident in which I suffered life-changing injuries, yet God sent a Christian woman to pray over my wrecked body and bleeding head. Testimony to the ways God heals. Demonstration of His deep, unending love for me. Confirmation that I am alive to tell my story. And His story.

Do you feel your scars still, whether old or new? Whether physical or emotional or an interfusion.

Maybe you would benefit from what I did. I decided to turn my wounds into wisdom. I took each scar and used it to help others. Not only that, but I turned my story into a testimony and the compassion I felt for others who had suffered pain also, became a key emotion and a reason for me to write, to share and to love. Maybe today you can picture scars upon

 your heart. Why not decide to turn the trauma into testimony. The damage into a demonstration of Christ's healing power. The anguish into an illustration of His redeeming love. After all, when you allow the healing to begin it isn't only your life that will change. Countless other lives are changed too.

You won't be the only one Ellie'vated.

You will Ellie'vate everyone you tell your story to!

Read ~ Psalm 147:3, Jeremiah 17:14, Psalm 107:20

Ellie'vation ~ Watch a Louie Giglio YouTube video called Indescribable. It will remind you of the greatness of God. A true Ellie'vation!

Ellie'vation

~

Lifting You

Up Above

Your

Situation!

Day 20

He is BIG!

Whatever is before you today, remember to

LOOK UP and don't forget that God is bigger than any problem, any trouble, any dispute, any dilemma, and any person!

But you've got to have faith!

You may be thinking, "But Ellie, I caused this mess myself!" Ah, well, that means you're facing a 'consequence.' Yes, I've faced lots of those too! God will still be there for you. He's still got you. He is STILL bigger than anything or anyone you are facing! The first thing you need to do if you know you're dealing with a consequence is repent, and ask God for mercy, grace, and help. Remind Him that He is bigger than what you are facing!

Next, trust!

But if you're dealing with a trial, and it came from nowhere then you have to *believe* that God has got this. You *need* to believe that. You need FAITH! This is what faith is! Believing He will come through for you.

On certain occasions in the past, the trouble comes thick and fast, and it's a trial all on its own. I haven't caused it. It's not a consequence of my own silly actions. It's just something I'm going to have to get through. I won't do that well if I don't have a strong faith in God.

Faith is *'the substance of things hoped for.'* It's *'the evidence of things not seen.'*

When God sees your incredible faith, He is moved to move! You have to believe! It's no use praying and not believing that God will come through for you. Despite previous situations, and irrespective of all preceding unanswered requests, today, you MUST have faith that He is bigger than your circumstance and believe you have the victory!

Do you know the story in the Bible about Bartimaeus the blind man?

Bartimaeus was sitting on the side of the road begging, probably for food and water. When he heard that Jesus was passing by, he started to cry out for Jesus to have mercy on him. All the other people in the crowds that were following Jesus and His disciples were threatening him to be quiet, yet this didn't stop him.

He cried out more for Jesus to help him. Jesus stopped and

asked for the man to be brought to him and Jesus asked him, *"What do you want me to do for you?"* Bartimaeus simply asked Jesus for his sight. Guess what Jesus said to him? *"Go your way; your FAITH has made you well."* And Bartimaeus instantly received sight!

It wasn't that Jesus first decided to do a miracle! He did the miracle *because* of the strength of faith Bartimaeus had! You've gotta have faith!

Be Ellie'vated right now knowing that the God who parted the Red Sea can make a way for you today where there seems to be no way.

Read ~ 1 Timothy 6:12, 2 Corinthians 5:7, Ephesians 6:16

Ellie'vation ~ Pay someone a compliment today. I love nothing more than the surprise, then smile on somebody's face when I comment on their dress, or their top, or I tell them their hair is shiny or their skin is glowing. It can Ellie'vate someone's whole day! And yours.

Day 21

There is no comparison!

I once shared a quote on my Instagram account that said, 'Too busy growing my own grass to notice if yours is greener.' And guess what? It's true! I'm so busy with my own life that I rarely have a minute to be worried about anybody else's life. I am concerned about the lives of the people in my church family, if, and when, they call on me to be concerned, and I am always interested and happy to hear about the lives of my friends and close friends who are considered family. But when would I find the time to be absorbed and engrossed in the life of Joe Bloggs at number 52 on the next street, or Susie on the second to the last row in a church of 2,000 that I'm only visiting to preach at? It can border on 'gossip', and it can cause comparison. And here is another quote that is well known and oh so true! 'Comparison is the thief of joy!' I agree, and whenever I have heard somebody compare their life with somebody else's life, it seems to make them so miserable!

I can clearly see that comparison is a thief of joy. When I look for examples in the Bible, I find them easily. God even alludes to it in the

Ten Commandments, **'Do not have a desire for your neighbour's house; do not have a desire for his wife............ or anything that belongs to your neighbour."** Exodus 20:17

When we measure ourselves against others it can create unnecessary divisions, grudges, resentments, bitterness and even malice.

But we should all want to be the best person we can possibly be because God made each of us in His image.

However, let's flip the script here! Instead of comparing yourself, why not emulate the praiseworthy, amiable, and most admirable features of people. Instead of wishing you had what they had, why not build up the beneficent qualities of their character in yourself and work on the constructive capabilities of you?!

Who inspires you to be a better you?

Imagine if you could Ellie'vate the comparison game into a useful tool for life!

Why not figure out the things you do well and determine not to fixate on others so much that it causes you to compare yourself resentfully. Our very own lifework, our pursuits, our gifts, vocations, and personal attributes are precious and set by God for us before even the foundations of the earth were set! You are *that* special!

Today, Ellie'vation in your life will come from you implementing a healthy, spiritual self-image that will lay the foundations for you to work in freedom for God! Don't compare yourself to others!

There is no comparison!

Read ~ 2 Corinthians 10:12, 2 Peter 1:1, Colossians 1:15

Ellie'vation ~ Listen to the song Transfiguration by Hillsong Worship. Put your earphones in and listen to the words closely. Be Ellie'vated!

Day 22

Health and Safety

It was quite possibly one of the most embarrassing bumps of my life!

A friend had asked me to nip into a flooring shop in order to provide her with an either positive or negative opinion on a carpet she was considering buying. My friends know I consider myself a bit of an interior design connoisseur, so I jumped at the chance to utilise my competent analysis in carpet composition!

The store building was very modern; so modern in fact, that it looked to me, to be almost open plan with a full open air foyer.

So I ran up the front steps to literally shoot in, make my decision, and then get out as quickly as possible and I very abruptly slammed into……..a hard mass! Yes! There was a door! A very large, very state-of-the-art, very see-through, door!

Physically, I'd really hurt myself because I had run up the steps fast, so I hit the 'invisible' door with full force, but the pain I felt most was humiliation. Oh my goodness! A lady came to check if I was ok, but I could see people inside sniggering. I was so embarrassed, even though, looking back it had to be a health and safety hazard! Hadn't other people done the same? They must have!

It really makes me think about the doors we come across in our lives.

The doors that open so easily.

The doors that are seemingly shut tight.

The doors we pray about; wanting God to open *more* doors!

I had wanted to go through that door at the carpet shop, but I hadn't even noticed it was shut. I'd presumed it was an open gateway for me to enter, but what seemed certain and real, actually wasn't! Because it was shut, and I galloped towards it, full force without care or concern, I *hurt* myself!

It was a spiritual lesson for me. I may think, due to my own fleshly desires and dreams, that a door is open, and I may ultimately set off, full steam ahead to get through that door. Images, dreams, and thoughts of what is waiting on the other side………

But unless I've prayed; unless I discern the steps in which God is directing me, I could SLAM into another hard mass! In fact, I have done this in the past.

But God………there we go………BUT GOD! He has a beautiful way of rubbing my bumps all better, inserting some wisdom into that (sore) head of mine and guiding me toward the appropriate door……..for me *and* for Him, at the perfect time.

This Ellie'vates me immediately. Knowing that He is ready and waiting to soothe my hurts with His healing balm. He is ready today to soothe yours, too.

Monsters Inc. is one of my favourite films ever! It is, to me, the 'wrap up in a duvet with popcorn and chocolate' type of film!

The best scene is the door chasing scene; Sulley and Mike, the two main character monsters, are riding a door whilst holding tight onto Boo, the little girl, amongst a rollercoaster ride of doors. They are looking for Boo's bedroom door as it has gone missing, and they need to find it, so she is able to get safely back home. At one point, they go through a door that leads to an appealing Caribbean beach and Mike is very tempted to stay there! And I can't blame him because it looks peaceful, tranquil, and free from strife.

But Sully says, "No! We have to find Boo's door!" It was the right door, the only door, for that time in their journey and basically the only one that would get Boo safely back to her home! Even though it all seemed perfect and dreamy and wonderful on the other side of the door that Mike went through, it wasn't the perfect place for Boo!

We are on a life journey, and on our way to getting home, our heavenly home, whilst travelling this earthly journey let's remember not to hang on to handles or doors that are locked to us; let's not run into seemingly open pathways because of our own wants and needs; getting *bumped* in the process!

And let's not try to close doors ourselves, that we know God has opened, for the reason that it looks too difficult. Don't block your blessings!

Read ~ Revelation 3:8, Colossians 4:3, Acts 14:27

Ellie'vation ~ Post some tracts, declaring the love of God and the salvation that Jesus offers, around your town or village. Or offer one next time you're out and start a conversation with someone you haven't spoken with before.

Day 23

It's all tied together

You were born at the exact time, in the exact place, to the exact parents that God planned. And God had it all tied together! YOU! Your life, your personality, your talents, your giftings, the way you look, even as you are reading this today! It's all tied together and wrapped up in an unequivocally, perfectly planned destiny, tailor-made for you!
You are exactly exact! You are the one and only! And that means one thing. You have an exclusive purpose too!

You don't need to concern yourself with worry that somebody else has stolen your position, or that job, or your girlfriend, or that husband, or this house. NOBODY can ever steal the blessings that God has ordained for you in the same way you cannot steal from anybody else blessings He has ordained for them!
And why would you want to?
What's yours is yours and what's theirs is theirs!

Nobody else on this earth has your abilities and talents which are mingled with your personality and position in life to do the job that God has called you to do.

In God's beautiful, magnificent, and perfect plan you have great value, great significance and there is a reason you were born. Not one person is born for nothing.

But I really believe that it's up to us to be obedient to God, and answer His call, in order for us to live a truly abundant life. If we want to ignore God and live life the opposite way to God's way, not following His instruction, then I believe we will miss out on our purpose and all the joy and satisfaction that comes with that.

Being obedient is the key.
Right now, even as you read this book, maybe you can't see it or feel it, but even now, God is preparing you, adapting situations and scenarios in your sphere of influence, adjusting plotlines, and positioning people, to accomplish all that He has marked you down for!

The next chapter is about to begin! Are you ready to turn the page?!

Remember! You are exactly exact! You are not a mistake. You are here because God wants you here. Just as God had a plan for every single person in the Bible, the ones we know with names and the ones mentioned whose names we never knew, God has a plan for you. An exact plan! King David said in Psalm 139:16, *"All the days ordained for me were written in your book before one of them came to be."*

To Ellie'vate you today let me share one more thought if you are struggling to celebrate YOU at the moment, and your uniqueness, and all that you are.
I know sometimes we hear the phrase, 'God doesn't make mistakes' and that is true. But have you ever thought what an insult it is to God when we moan about things we don't like about ourselves, or we don't appreciate the skills and talents He has given us, or we want to have, or be, someone else instead of ourselves? It's almost like we're saying to God, "You've got it wrong."
Whoa! God doesn't get His creation wrong ever! You are made perfectly in His image and exactly the way He wanted you to be made.

Love your uniqueness. Thank God for it! And let's learn to love the uniqueness in others too.
Open your eyes to the exquisiteness of God in every person you meet today.

It's all tied together.

Read ~ Matthew 10:29-31, Ephesians 2:10, Psalm 139:13-16

Ellie'vation ~ Collect all of your photographs from your phone and computer and have everything put into albums for each year. You can find some great companies online that make it easy for you to just upload the pictures, and the albums are made and sent through the post.

Day 24

The measure of your compassion

What does Ellie'vation have to do with being

a compassionate person? The answer is……. a lot! When you think of someone who is compassionate, do you associate it with somebody who has a martyr type character? Unfortunately, in the world we live in, some people do. Compassionate people can be seen as soft or weak. But as a Christian, I see it not only a strength, but as a duty to be compassionate. And I can't help it, anyway! To me, compassion is a superpower!

A big lesson I have learned throughout the course of my life is to have a ton of compassion for others and a lot of compassion for myself too. And that's what I want to share with you today, to Ellie'vate you today, to remind you today that you are worthy of compassion too, and to discover the measure of our compassion.

People who emulate compassion both to themselves and for others have learned the art of not taking things too personally. They know that when a mistake happens, that is simply a fact – a mistake happened. They don't focus on how much of a failure they are, or the other person is, or how stupid they feel, or labelling anyone else who made a mistake. They simply focus on correcting the mistake, if able, and don't internalise it as being about themselves.

Since compassionate people practice self-compassion as well as compassion for others, they can move forward quickly. They don't hold grudges. They don't constantly ruminate, worry, and incessantly chatter about the problem. I remember when I used to have so little compassion for myself and turned myself inside out with angst if I felt I had offended somebody in the slightest way! I don't do that anymore. I have learnt to show the same compassion to myself as I give to others and it's the healthiest thing you can do!

When you have experienced excessive emotional and physical pain it gives you clear insight and an amazing vantage point to problem-solve for others who are suffering. I remember my grandfather couldn't bear to see people suffering. He was such a compassionate man. He said to me when I was tiny, "If everyone was like Jesus, this world would be a better place." I like to think he is watching me now, trying my best every day to be more Christlike.

But what's the measure of our compassion? How far does it go? Does our compassion stretch to the unloveliest of people? To our enemies?

> In Luke 6:32-36 Jesus said, **"If you love those who love you, what credit is that to you? Even 'sinners' love those who love them. And if you do good to those who are good to you, what credit is that to you? Even 'sinners' do the same......But love your enemies, do good, and lend, hoping for nothing in return; and your reward will be great, and you will be sons of the Most High, because He is kind to the unthankful and evil. Therefore be merciful, just as your Father is also merciful."**

I have to remember that God first called me when I was unlovable. He showed true compassion to me. It wasn't based on who I was, what I did, where I lived or how much I knew. It wasn't even based on whether I deserved it! God's compassion and love for me is unconditional. And that is the measure He wants me to show to others.

Realise the tremendous strength you have when you can show compassion to others in this broken world. Go out and use your superpower!

Ellie'vate someone else today!

What's the measure of your compassion?

Read ~ Romans 12:15, 1 Peter 3:8, Ephesians 4:32

Ellie'vation ~ Give somebody a call today to see if they need help with anything. There are so many people who don't ask for help and a lot of the time, the people who look like they have it all together are falling apart at the seams behind closed doors. So, have a think who you could call, and Ellie'vate someone else today!

Day 25

We need to talk about forgiveness

Some of my most fulfilling

conversations are with people who are looking for answers. 'Why do I have to forgive someone who caused me so much pain?' 'How do I forgive someone who caused me so much pain?' 'How can people lie so much and get away with it?' 'I thought they were Christians!?' 'They were my parents!' 'We were best friends!' 'They were such gossips!'

The list goes on and on and on……

People will always hurt people. It has been happening since the beginning of time. People who you know and people who you don't know can say nasty comments about you, people in the world and in the workplace will gossip about you, people will always be jealous and envious of others, someone will always want what they think you have…… It's a never-ending and heartbreaking wheel of nastiness, but it never stops turning. And you must decide whether you allow it to circle around your mind for the rest of your days, or not. I decided a while ago to let go. Let go of the things people had said and done to me and stop anything coming out of someone else's lips and into my ears about anybody else!

The only opinion I care about is the opinion of God. If He knows what is happening in my life, then that's all that matters. If someone wants to say nasty things about me, well, to be honest, I don't really care. It says more about them than me.

At times, I have been able to spiritually see the venom pour through the skin of people with a spirit of envy, and it makes me feel so sad for them. It must be awful to go through life never really concentrating on your own life and all the amazing things that you could be doing, because you allow yourself to become overly obsessed with someone else. When I have prayed at the time, God has shown me the outcome, and that I needed to pray for them even more.

Yet as I look at some of these lives currently, they are still in the same places, spiritually, probably being jealous and eaten up inside about others now. What a waste of a life!

This is what happens if you are full of unforgiveness or resentment or bitterness for others.

It doesn't help anyone. Not you, not them, not anyone!

Forgiving someone who has persecuted you is worth it. It is worth it for you and for them. Everyone implicated gains in one way or another. You may feel like you benefit poorly because you were the person originally wounded, but you will not benefit at all by not forgiving.

At its essence, forgiveness is not about the other person particularly when the wrongdoing is extreme. What they did might have been appalling, but when you forgive you are being totally obedient to God, and He will honour that. He knows that forgiving others supports the healing you need, and it helps you find peace.

When you forgive others, it becomes simpler to forgive yourself too. Grace has a highly contagious effect just like laughter. Generally, when we pinpoint our thoughts and comprehend how animosity, bitterness and hurts affect us when they are about other people, we can also notice how those same views affect us when they are about things we find difficult to forgive ourselves for. When you forgive *them*, it becomes much easier to forgive *yourself.*

Let it go! Today, forgive anyone and everyone that ever hurt you.

And you will feel yourself rising higher....

You will absolutely feel Ellie'vated!

Read ~ Luke 6:37, Acts 13:38, Acts 3:19

Ellie'vation ~ Bake bread or a cake for an elderly person in your neighbourhood. They will really appreciate it!

Day 26

We still need to talk about forgiveness

It is embedded in my mind that I will be judged if I judge others. Put conversationally; it freaks me out!!

You may find I mention the topics of forgiveness and resentment more than twice in this book. Let me explain why. I believe getting rid of the feelings and emotions attached to these divisional themes is the doorway to freedom, and it's a mission of mine to share with others. Not just the key to emotional freedom, but to relational freedom and strong physical health too.

People who are able to forgive have a more cheerful and contented perspective on life. They can see that forgiveness isn't just the righteous thing to do, but it's also a gift to themselves.

I know exactly how it feels when you're struggling to forgive someone who hasn't shown any remorse for their actions but that's where God's grace enters. When you get on your knees and ask God to help you forgive, even the worst of betrayals, I can promise you He will. Our mighty God will pour out His grace upon you and it will aid you and comfort you as you lay your interior pain at the foot of the Cross.

God wants you to give that pain to Him. He promises that if you do, vengeance belongs to Him. Look at it like this. Whenever I have a mountain of work to do and a friend offers to take a ton of it away to lighten my load, I can breathe. I feel lighter, and I am free to carry hope that I will get to the other side of this mountain!

It's the same with letting go of the emotions connected to unforgiveness. You cannot relish life and appreciate the joy in your days if you are filled to the brim with unforgiveness, resentment and bitterness.

When you've been wounded and damaged by somebody, in particular, by someone you rely on, believe in, and put all your trust in, it can cause utter devastation.

And one of the main things that prevents people from forgiving is unresolved anger. They feel like the person who isn't remorseful is getting away with their painful actions but that's not what forgiveness is about. Forgiving someone doesn't mean you disregard their conduct. But to impede further emotional damage to you, to stop being the victim and become

the victor, forgiving the person, whether they are remorseful or not, releases you to get on with the next chapter of your life. They are part of the past. Why bring them into the next scene? How many 'today's' do you have? Why squander your 'today' being preoccupied with bitter animosities?

To Ellie'vate yourself today embrace this present moment! Let go of the former times, the bygone days, the people who let you down. Prevail so you can be fully present in the present!

Read ~ Daniel 9:9, Galatians 6:1, Hebrews 4:16

Ellie'vation ~ Listen to the song Heaven Invade by Kari Jobe. Another one to listen to very loud! Feel the emotion.

Day 27

It's none of your business

It's not your business or my business what anybody says about us or thinks about us. That's between them and God.

Think about that.

Caring about what other people think about you borders on pride. It's wasting time filling your mind and your thoughts with information which is of no benefit to you. It isn't teaching you anything. It isn't causing you joy or peace. We have around 10,000 thoughts every day and I want 10,000 worthwhile things to be thinking about! If someone else wants to be having 10,000 thoughts about me, well, enjoy!

It's no coincidence that God made sure the Bible contained scriptures regarding our mind and our thoughts!

"And do not be conformed to this world, but be transformed by the renewing of your mind, that you may prove what is that good and acceptable and perfect will of God." Romans 12:2

"Finally, brethren, whatever things are true, whatever things are noble, whatever things are just, whatever things are pure, whatever things are lovely, whatever things are of good report, if there is any virtue and if there is anything praiseworthy – meditate on these things." Philippians 4:8

Our brain and our mind are incredible, extraordinary gifts from God. Consider this. If we have an unhealthy mind, we struggle to go about our day. When we have mental health challenges it affects every area of our lives, so it's imperative we keep our mind and our thoughts as healthy as possible!

A few years ago (I've mentioned in another devotional in this book), I was involved in an almost fatal road accident. I suffered a traumatic brain injury which wasn't dealt with correctly initially, and I have been living with the fall out of this for the last few years. It's been tough, very tough. The thing with brain injuries, head injuries and mental health challenges is they are invisible illnesses. People don't see the injury on you or view the actual sickness you are struggling with and unfortunately cannot understand the depth of any pain or issues you may be living with. I had been living in what felt like

an endless season of pain, misunderstanding and loss.

However, as I fill my mind with what is true and of good report, what is lovely and praiseworthy, as I think on only the good outcome, I can focus on God's promises and believe for a better future.

Let's Ellie'vate ourselves today by marvelling at the goodness of God and His gifts. Let's not fill our minds with rubbish. Let's not concern ourselves with people who moan or gossip.

Let's go about our Father's business and our own.

Read ~ Philippians 2:5, Philippians 4:8, 1 Corinthians 14:15

Ellie'vation ~ Write a list of 5 things you are looking forward to. Write another list of 5 things you are grateful for.

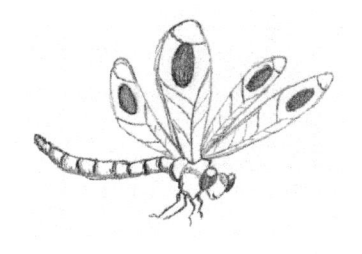

Day 28

I Smile

"I LIKE SMILING!"

That was my response to somebody the other day as they questioned, "Ellie, how come you're always smiling?"

I should share further.

The fact is I cannot help smiling!

I smile when I wake up……..because I woke up! Praise God!

I smile when I taste my first cup of coffee!

I smile when my dog flies onto the bed with joy because I'm awake!

I smile because I have a blessed life! Why shouldn't I smile…..a lot! I forgive, I love, I pray I care, I do……..I smile!

I can hear you now as you read this, "Nobody can be that happy all the time."

And let me tell you. If you'd been where I've been you'd smile a lot too!

> **"Therefore, I say to you, her sins, which are many, are forgiven, for she loved much. But to whom little is forgiven, the same loves little."** Luke 7:47

At any rate, it isn't necessarily about happiness. It isn't about your mood or circumstance. Nope! It's about *that* moment and whether or not you choose to be optimistic or pessimistic.

But my favourite time to smile is when I'm praying......I'm communicating with my Father in heaven......I just drink in all His love......and smile.

There have been times in my life when smiling would seem impossible. But you know, even in the worse times of my life I would unintentionally invite favour into my life, because of my smile.

Smiling can introduce a connection, an opening. It's a way of reaching people; a way of displaying you care too! A couple of years ago I was ministering about the love of Jesus to some destitute children in the gypsy villages of Transylvania, Romania. Some of the children depicted feelings of unworthiness and wouldn't join in with others. They didn't wear appropriate clothing for the freezing temperatures, or even footwear due to the poverty their families endured. It was heartbreaking and all I wanted to do was love them, involve them, and hug them. I gave the children the biggest, warmest smile I could, and they came to me. They accepted the love I was offering. They responded to my smile. We couldn't speak each other's language but that didn't matter, did it?

Because a smile is universal!

You can smile in any language! Every person in the world understands a smile!

Do you know!? If you're feeling miserable, overwhelmed, or downright heartbroken I can guarantee if you look in a mirror and just smile, you will instantly alter your brain physically! You can trick yourself into feeling brighter by influencing your brain activity with a grin! And that affects your health and well-being, your heart rate relaxes, and your blood pressure reduces! (And let's face it, if you're smiling at yourself in the bathroom mirror, trying to improve your mood, you *have* to laugh, never mind smile!)

Plus, don't you just love being around people who make you smile? It can be tough spending time with someone who seems intent on being as miserable as possible, or who seems to look on life as 'a glass half empty'. We're all made perfectly imperfectly and I'm thankful that God gave each of us such diverse personalities, but I love that God gave me the personality to generate a smile, in others and myself!

Additionally, what blows my mind is that our Father in Heaven, our amazing God, smiles upon us! He looks at you and me and He smiles! Doesn't *that* make you want to beam from ear to ear?

"There are many who say, "Who will show us any good?" Lord, lift up the light of your countenance upon us." Psalm 4:6

Lord Byron wrote, *'Be thou the rainbow in the storms of life. The evening beam that smiles the clouds away, and tints tomorrow with prophetic ray.'*

If I can Ellie'vate you in any way today, I hope it's the above way.

And I pray right now for you, the reader,

"If you're feeling down, let me pray for you, I'll be a rainbow in this storm.

If you're in a dark place, let me pray for you, I'll be an evening beam that smiles those clouds away.

If you're sad today and dreading tomorrow, let me pray for you and hopefully tint tomorrow with prophetic prayer."

Read ~ Proverbs 31:25, Psalm 34:5, Proverbs 15:30

Ellie'vation ~ Listen to one of my favourite songs of all time, I Smile, by Kirk Franklin. It will Ellie'vate your mood instantly! Even my dog, George, loves this song, and there he is below! Always making me smile!

Day 29

This too shall pass

I repeat, this too shall pass. Isn't it just the way that during those peak times of prosperity, peace of mind and utter jubilation, those times when absolutely everything is going just great, we remember that nothing ever stays the same? We start to dwell on the transitory nature of each season in life and wonder when this elation and time of massive blessing might end.

Yet, when we're going through tough times, we think it's never going to end! We're persuaded beyond doubt that this is it forever! We decide bad times are what we should get used to!

Conversely, knowing that 'this too shall pass' whenever we are journeying through unsettled seasons and keeping it in firmly in mind is the most helpful thing you can do for yourself! Meditate on this.

Probably because I'm at the middle-aged part of my life (!) I now have the beautiful benefit of hindsight so I can Ellie'vate you today by sharing the following.

Looking at the bigger picture and not just at this snapshot in time *proves* to us all that 'this too shall pass.' You only have to recall previous events and situations in your life to know that this current situation you may want to end is just one sentence in a paragraph, or one paragraph in a chapter. And any minute now, you're about to start a brand new chapter on a brand new page! So, hold on and remember that time is the panacea for tough seasons and your current circumstances are not the way things are forever, they're just the way things are *this minute*.

Very soon you will be in a period of Ellie'vation!

I know it!

Read ~ 2 Corinthians 4:17-18, Matthew 24:35, 1 John 2:17

Ellie'vation ~ Decide to spend one month taking a small step each day towards a goal. Maybe you could eat one extra piece of fruit every day for a month, or a carrot every day, or commit to drinking a litre of water every day. Maybe decide to train with dumbbells with a home workout. If you don't normally do this you'll notice a huge difference. Start small and see what happens! But pick a goal and stick to it!

Day 30

Don't Look Back

You have the biggest smile on your face

today! You opened this book and you're thinking, "I'm not even sure I need to read a devotional today because I'm already Ellie'vated!!" Although maybe there is a little niggle, a tiny annoying thought popping up every now and then, a bothersome rumination……Hmmm, yes, I do need a little Ellie'vation! Maybe today you're in your Promised Land and it's a touch uncomfortable, or maybe you're in the wilderness and you know you've become way too cosy!

Let me help you now. Don't leave your Promised Land just because you're uncomfortable. Don't evacuate the area! Don't give up and never give in! Because if you are in your Promised Land, the place you've been praying to get to, it's always going to be preferable to the wilderness!

So many people spend so long in the wilderness seasons of their lives that they become complacent in their prayer lives, they become comfortable in the not knowing, and they become contented with the mediocre. They gave up on their Promised Land many seasons ago. God didn't give up on them! They gave up on God! And it was so subtle they didn't even realise!

A little unpleasantness or some hardship certainly isn't proof that you've made an inaccurate choice or taken the wrong direction because you *already* know you prayed for where you are now. When life feels tough in your Promised Land it's because you've got to develop and expand in brand new ways, far bigger and far wider than you ever reached before, over and above your previous constraints. God has taken you to another level. He takes us from glory to glory!

I bet you're glad you kept reading today, aren't you?!

The Promised Land may have giants to overcome and new love languages to learn, it may have routes and roads you need to discover, and fresh connections you need to action, but God is right there with you, not only cheering you on because you finally got to the place He wanted you to be, but because He wants you to have an abundantly joy filled life and He

knows this is the spacious place where you will glorify His name! He's got this! So don't look back to the comfortable wilderness. Don't be Lot's wife!! Looking back only caused destruction. For her and her family.

Move on ahead. Keep looking forward and seize the day!

Now that's some serious Ellie'vation!

Read ~ Proverbs 16:1-4, Matthew 6:25-34, Jeremiah 29:11

Ellie'vation ~ Make a vision board. Print out pictures and texts of the goals and dreams you have and are praying for. I did this years ago and apart from one thing, each desire has happened through prayer and faith. Some seemed impossible. It's the impossible things that we need the most faith for, to believe in the vision from God. And that one thing I am waiting on will still happen, I truly believe! I wait in anticipation!

Day 31

Find your tribe

Who are the people you hang around with the most?

I think we tend to have a specific group of friends who we go out to eat with, or grab coffee with, or in my case, I love an afternoon tea, especially Earl Grey tea and a huge plate of scones with jam and clotted cream. Oh dear! I shouldn't have started writing that! It's not time for a break yet……

Ok, I'm back!

It's said that we are the sum total of the five people we surround ourselves with the most. Therefore, a key factor in living a life of Ellie'vation and maintaining a joyful existence is to endeavour to make sure that group of people, your tribe shall we say, are the best kind of people for you and that you can be the best kind of friend for them.

We need friends that will help us to flourish and mature spiritually and will encourage us and spur us on when it feels like life is really beating us up. I honestly don't know where I would be if it wasn't for my incredible friends! God has always blessed me profoundly around friendships and for that I'm ever thankful. I love to be a good friend too and I hope I am!

I believe the right kind of friends are the ones who would hold you accountable if they felt you were going down a wrong path. I want those kinds of friends! A friend who would say, "Hang on a minute, lady! If you think I'm going to stand by and watch this scenario you've got another thing coming…….." THAT friend!

Relationships and friendships are so valuable to God, and He wants them to be valuable to us. I have built a wonderful network of love around my daughter and I with our friends and church family. We feel blessed.

To Ellie'vate yourself today why not compose a list of all the people in your life, your own network of love, and endeavour to hold them up in prayer. You'll soon discover God answering some of those prayers in the most mind-blowing of ways!

Do you know that as soon as Job prayed for his friends God re-established his fortunes? It's one of those scriptures and stories from the Bible that has always stayed with me. He prayed for his friends and God not only **'restored his prosperity but DOUBLED his former possessions.'**

Now, I'm not suggesting you pray for your network of love, your tribe, your friends, in order to receive brilliant blessings from the Lord, although that's always nice. I'm reminding you just how important God sees it that we pray for our friends!

So evidently, our tribe is significant. Our love structure of buddies is crucial. Our companions are imperative.

Let's all aim to be trustworthy, encouraging, understanding, considerate, thoughtful, joyful, and forgiving!

Be the best tribe member you can be!

Read ~ Proverbs 17:9, Proverbs 27:9, Job 16:20-21

Ellie'vate ~ Buy a book for a friend. A book about friendship, a book about something that means a lot to them, maybe one of their hobbies, maybe buy them a devotional like this one. Pop a lovely note inside to let them know you chose the book because you love them, and they mean so much to you!

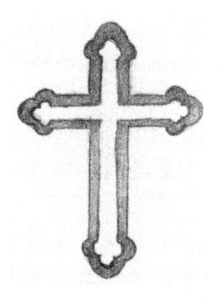

Day 32

It's Never Too Late

We all mess up. We all make mistakes. Sadly, this can lead to us opening a door to fear. Today, we can Ellie'vate our whole day by discovering how to obtain freedom from the fear that we can never get things right ever again!

Do you know the story about King David when he had to escape from people who were out to kill him? He was in obvious danger! He had to vanish as fast as he could, but he landed straight into the hands of another enemy! The Philistines in Gath. Furthermore, the reason he was in this situation was because he had made some thoughtless and irrational decisions in the first place. Does that remind you of anyone? Because it undeniably reminds me of some seasons in my life.

The decisions aren't the length of a season…. but boy oh boy! The consequences are! And sometimes even beyond a season.

So, David was a fugitive and landed in a place deemed as unsafe because Gath was considered a land of unbelievers and whilst David was there it was regarded as outside the protection and blessing of

God. Because David initially acknowledged only his fear, and didn't turn to God for help, his only thought was to run, thus causing himself to dive right into a further convoluted, entangled, complex mess!

Hands up! Been there! Got the T-shirt! Don't plan on wearing it ever again though!

And all of this because of his own hasty and reckless decisions to begin with!

He is running scared of Saul and his men. He is frightened of the Philistines. There are enemies coming at him from pretty much every direction! He pretends to act like a madman to get away from them and he's doubtless humiliated at having to look like a deranged clown before all his adversaries.

Nevertheless, David determines to finally behave based on God's character, not on his own fear, his despair and trepidation.

In Psalm 56, we read David's account of this time, and how eventually he does turn to God for help.

And this is what I want to share with you today.

This is where the most beautiful Ellie'vation is. This is how wonderful our God is. This is how deep His love is for us.

David resolves to embrace his faith undeterred by his own mistakes and the intimidations of his enemies. Possibly David wrote this psalm as he travelled back to Israel. He's reflecting over recent events and again, pursuing God for reassurance, guidance, and comfort. King David irrefutably knows the faithfulness and benevolence of God.

Despite all the mess, the mix up, the mayhem, David asks God to save him from his enemies, from the ramifications of his *own dreadful decisions*. He chose faith over fear.

And God does rescue him.

God will do the same for you. You may feel you have left it too late to ask Him for help. You haven't. I can assure you as sure as I can tell you that the sun will set tonight! It's never too late with our God.

You may feel too ashamed to ask Him to deliver you from your burden. That feeling is a lie from the pit of hell. He never wants you to feel shame. Rebuke that feeling now, in the Name of Jesus!

God is full of benevolence, grace, forgiveness, and love. Every bad decision you have made can be turned around for good, if you give it to Him now and trust Him. I really believe that, because I have experienced it and I've seen what He can do in my own life.

Be Ellie'vated today by trusting in God's promises, not by trusting in your mistakes.

Read ~ Acts 2:38, 2 Chronicles 7:14, 2 Peter 3:9

Ellie'vation ~ Is there a character trait about someone in your circle of influence that you don't like? How about you look for one thing about them that you do like and highlight it to them? Let them know how much you appreciate that part of their personality and see what happens!

Day 33

What do you see?

Whenever I look ahead and figure out what must happen before I attain a goal I want to reach, I look into a space. Because that's all there is to see right at that moment. Do I fill it with worry, doubt, angst, and fear? Or do I fill it with optimism, vision, and focus-filled faith!

God fills empty spaces. And nothing in this world can fill the empty spaces in your life the way He can. Tragically, we live in a world where it is easy to fill ourselves up brim-full with the pleasures of this world, and those pleasures are tipping out before we can make any room for God.

If you're hoping to pursue a goal and you have a vision for the future, make sure the space you're looking into has a foundation of faith in God, a bedrock of confidence in Jesus and that you are willing to accept His will no matter what.

Do you want to be in any space where God isn't? I don't.

I want every space I am in, I am heading for, to be a God space.

I am assured that wherever I am, God is in that space with me. But I also

think that there are spaces where we are more purposeful in our endeavours and determinations in positioning ourselves to have a conscious acknowledgement of God's presence, whether we are in our prayer closet at home, in church, at a mid-week prayer meeting or away at a conference.

However, what about the spaces and places where the majority of the world wouldn't believe God hovers over. War torn countries with bomb attacked houses, famine hit villages in third world countries, railway track bridges covering tin can fires surrounded with huddled homeless, streets with freezing cold girls in short skirts, standing on corners battered and bruised, waiting for work in cars. Is God in that space?

Yes.

Whenever I look ahead and figure out what must happen before I attain a goal I want to reach, I look into a space. Because that's all there is to see right at that moment. Do I fill it with worry, doubt, angst, and fear? Or do I fill it with optimism, vision, and focus-filled faith!

He sent me.

He sent you.

He is there.

Ellie'vate another today.

Read ~ Habakkuk 1:5, Zechariah 5:5, Mark 8:25

Ellie'vation ~ Listen to the song Spirit Lead Me by Hillsong United. As you listen pray and meditate on the words.

Day 34

Who are you listening to?

When the enemy murmurs in your ear, "You'll never do this, it's because he never wants you to do it! There are so many negative remarks I hear Christians speaking about themselves day in and day out. I believe it's because they are listening to the wrong thoughts! The enemy loves when we believe his lies because he doesn't have to work as hard to mess things up for us.

Even so, the minute you do that, you're losing the power you have within you, which is the power of the Holy Spirit. Don't allow your mind and thoughts to establish the enemy's lies!

Establish God's Word in your mind! The enemy has spent the majority of his miserable fallen time trying to discredit God's Word and manipulating humans to doubt God's Word and God's promises to us.

He coaxes us to only view our obstacles, measure our difficulties and weigh our burdens when we should be focusing on God's abundant promises. God has made hundreds of incredible promises in His Word to us and will keep every promise because He cannot lie. Yet, how, and why do we continue to believe the enemy so easily when we know he is a liar?!

It's because it is easy to give in.

To draw on your strength emotionally, mentally, and physically, when you are feeling low, or overwhelmed can be difficult. It's a key juncture for the opposition to mutter defeatist commentary into your ear, but this is when you must take a stand and show your faith in God and His Word.

It is your faith which attracts the blessing of God. It is the taking captive of your thoughts that nullifies the enemy's hold on your immediate future.

Ellie'vate your thoughts today by reminding yourself to have the mind of Christ. It's your choice.

Read ~ 1 Corinthians 1:30, Hosea 6:6, John 14:26

Ellie'vation ~ Move your body and mend your mind! Every time you do a form of exercise, whether running on the spot, lifting some weights, stretching, walking around the block, kicking a ball, playing table tennis, doing a home exercise class, whatever it is, you instantly Ellie'vate your mood, and change your mindset. So move!

Day 35

Tiny Action – Huge Impact

Do you remember how you felt when you had a bad day and a stranger smiled at you? Or the times when a neighbour has helped you carry your shopping in the house or get your car off the drive when it's a time of icy weather? Each one of these tiny acts of kindness make a big impact on our lives, don't they?

Small actions lead to giant ripples! One small action can completely change the life of someone who then performs a kindness for someone else. And that cycle continues and grows! No matter how big or small the kindness is it's likely to have a big impact on your own mental health too! Research says that even the tiniest acts of kindness that we engage in can create a rebound effect, not only on the receiver's psyche but on your own too! I love this!

As an illustration, when you smile at someone, it increases their level of comfort along with making them feel happier. And it puts us in a better mood too. That simple smile could be the one thing that lifts somebody out of a pit of despair. It happened to me!

Tiny acts of kindness can make a change in 2 ways. They are a catalyst for others to start invoking their own small kindnesses and they have a contagious effect on others! In other words, when we carry out a little act of kindness, other people might see us doing them, and that inspires them!

Another instance is if you are friendly to the taxi driver, he then in turn will be more likely to be more considerate to his next passenger. That passenger is more likely to go home and have a positive conversation with their family. And do you know? People who tend to do small things to spread kindness are more likely to take action in bigger ways as well!

In Hebrew, the word for God's covenant kindness is 'chesed' and it means an aspect of grace, benevolence, mercy, or compassion and actually refers to the voluntary compulsion to give and to love without limit.

In Greek, the word for kindness is 'chrastos' and it means an attribute of integrity, morality,

goodness, graciousness and is action toward someone to furnish what is needed.

In Galatians 5:22-23 it says, **"But the fruit of the Spirit is love, joy, peace, longsuffering, kindness, goodness, faithfulness, gentleness, self-control. Against such there is no law."**

Kindness is one of the fruits of the Spirit. It's intended to be a sure sign, an endorsement almost, of being a Christian, of how we live our lives. It isn't an elective virtue. Having said that, Godly kindness doesn't come consistently to some people. So how do we transform into kind people? By permitting the Holy Spirit to help and refine us. But the Holy Spirit will only come into our lives when we welcome Him. He won't just voluntarily operate in the life of a Christian. And a transformed life only evolves as we submit to the Holy Spirit.

You will have a huge impact on your own mental health today as you do one small thing for another of God's children. And it won't be hard because God's children are everywhere! There's always someone waiting for a smile.

Ellie'vate someone today with YOUR smile and see where it leads.

Read ~ Galatians 5:22, 1 Peter 4:8, Ephesians 4:29

Ellie'vation ~ If you're able to, pay for the shopping of a customer in front of you at the local shop, or buy the coffee for the person in the line behind you. These little acts of kindness are never forgotten and can definitely Ellie'vate someone's day!

Day 36

The best defence

Have you ever felt as though the whole world was against you? Have you felt that everybody and everything was out to get you, and nothing was ever going to change? Those are pretty rough times and I think most people have endured periods like that at one time or another.

Out of the blue it seems, we can get our feelings hurt and immediately we may feel a surge of exasperation, and this can inflame the following conversation: it's almost as if the enemy has granted us the fortuity to be offended. A right to feel aggrieved.

But that's no way to Ellie'vate your mood! That's no way to lift you above a miserable situation!

Have you ever prayed to God and asked Him to help you see things in a different light? I've noticed in the past that it can be incredibly easy to misinterpret the intended meaning of other's words and yet our focus on the negative can magnify those words. Our minds run over and over the conversation, the situation, and unfortunately instead of scrambling to God, for peace, we scramble to judgement, for pain.

We care too much about what other people are saying about us or thinking about us. We pity ourselves whilst concurring that our 'enemy' is the sinner. Maybe they are painting us in a less than flattering light. Maybe someone is speaking untruths about you. But reacting to it……….?

Where does any of this get us?

Nowhere. It's a dead end road.

Reject that slippery slope down to self-pity and misery and remember that God is your defender!

Jesus never defended Himself. He never wasted a breath on those who had already made up their mind about who *they* thought He was. He didn't try to persuade them to like Him or change their minds about Him. He didn't argue back and forth or discuss the confrontation with other friends and see what they thought. He didn't do any of these things.

I imagine He didn't give the people who talked about Him behind His back, or argued with Him to His face, a second thought.

And that is our example. That is our Ellie'vation.

We do not need to safeguard ourselves when we are verbally persecuted, besieged, and wronged. Because God is our defender.

You will likely sense that God has helped you look at things in a different light and look at others in a different way, when you remain still, when you remain hushed and desire not to advocate for yourself. That day will come. And it brings peace. It brings freedom.

Because you know you need say nothing, as God is your defender!

Read ~ 2 Samuel 22:3, Psalm 3:3, Exodus 23:22

Ellie'vation ~ Listen to the song Defender – Sung by Steffany Gretzinger – Bethel Music

Day 37

Did you check the oil and water?

Did you check the oil and water? That was my response to a friend who rang me one day and said, "I really need to buy a new car; mine is smoking!"
I knew she didn't mean smoking hot, as she's been referring to the demise of this vehicle for months!
!Well, did you? Check the oil and water? Fill her up! It always works for me!"

Now any mechanics, or even anyone in general who knows a thing or two about cars, are now thinking, "What? Just keep the oil and water topped up and the car will be fine. That's not right! There's more to car maintenance than checking the oil and water!"

But seriously, it has always worked for me!

Mechanically and spiritually.

I have, over the years, owned many cars. I've owned some top of the range cars; received mediocre vehicles; acquired transit vans; enjoyed 2 high-powered sports cars; steered 7 ton lorries; relished a soft-top Jeep and utilised an SUV. I should really be given the opportunity to present an episode of Top Gear; not only one of my top 5 television programmes, but also a dream that I plan on becoming reality. How? I'm not sure right now, but whenever I commit a dream to God He always comes through! Because it's not just that I believe in Him. He believes in me too!

I religiously (got to love that word), check the oil and water in my car and pretty much always have done. My grandfather taught me this. He was a driving instructor and always maintained his cars to the utmost level. However, I only really observed the checking of oil and water and anticipated this to be the way forward. I thought checking the oil and water was the answer to all matters regarding the smooth functioning of a vehicle!

Here's my 30 year old standard checklist.

1. Check the oil and water monthly.
2. If there's a noise in the car, add oil, add water.
3. If there's a smell, add oil, add water.
4. If there's a ticking noise, add oil, add water.
5. If you swerve around a corner, add oil, add water, maybe check the tyres.

I firmly believe that if my lovely friend had just replenished the oil and water, she wouldn't have had to invest in a new vehicle. In fact, when I initially questioned her regarding oil and water, she admitted the following, "Oh, I never put oil and water in my car." (!!)

If you don't check or change the oil in your car, it *will* eventually affect your engine!
If you don't check the water level in the radiator, it *will* eventually

affect your engine!

And it's the same with us!

What are the levels of 'Living Water' like in your vehicle? In your body? In your heart?
We need to keep our levels high. Why? Because you never know when you're going to need to draw from that well of Living Water. If there isn't much of the Word inside you; if there isn't much of Jesus inside you; if the Living Waters are rapidly dissipating and you're not filling up on more of God's Word, more of the precious Living Water, then you're going to affect your engine. And once your engine is affected, other parts of your body; your vehicle, are going to be impaired also!

"Jesus answered and said to her, "If you knew the gift of God, and who it is who says to you, 'Give me a drink, 'you would have asked Him, and He would have given you living water.' "John 4:10

And how is your relationship with the Holy Spirit? Have you spoken to Him lately? Have you asked for a fresh and new anointing? Are you drenched in the oil of joy? Can people see the oil poured out upon you?

To Ellie'vate your heart, your body, and your mindset today, press into God and preserve your engine with the right oil and the right water.

The Holy Spirit. Jesus. Our Father.

Check the spiritual levels of oil and water in your life daily.

Check the number of a local garage.

DON'T use my check list.

Read ~ Psalm 133:2, James 5:14, Isaiah 61:3

Ellie'vation ~ Get organised!

Today make sure each part of your life is in order. The best way to Ellie'vate your mood is by getting 'all your ducks in a row!' When we get organised it lifts the stress that chaos can bring. So, clean out your kitchen drawers, give your old clothes to the charity shop, file away your paperwork, and plan your diary for the week.

Day 38

Split second thoughts – Lifelong memories

I recall a time when I was in New York, visiting the head office of the charity I worked for, but I was also partaking in ministry work whilst there. The organisation reached over 100,000 children every single week globally, not only with the Gospel of Christ, but with love, physical provision and basically whatever needs were necessary in the life of a child. One of the programmes was called visitation. This was where the staff would visit every single child that utilised the organisation; we were able to see if they were ok that week

and check if they or their families were in need of anything. We'd invite them to the next Sidewalk Sunday School or Indoor Sunday School and generally spend what time we could with them.

Because of the children we were trying to help, we would visit some of the poorest areas of cities all over the world. On this particular visit of mine, I was in the projects of Harlem, a place I have visited before on occasion and where I actually felt my heart led me. I want to point out, before I write of my personal experience, that I know some very special people living in the

projects: parents who really love their children and want to do their best for them. In fact, I could go so far as to say, I am their friend. Because I love them.

But in other areas of the projects, I would come across the depths of degradation. And when I knocked on some doors, I would be so *thankful* that God chose me to reach that child.
Around that time I had been writing my first book, Broken to Blooming, and I'd had to recall some distressing and harrowing incidents in my life; times I had locked away in the deepest recesses of my mind; but as the book was to be a testimony to as many as hopefully read it, I had to make a decision. Only the whole truth will do for God. Only the whole truth will show and prove that God has a plan for each and every life that is birthed on this earth.

The thing about writing down your own story is not only do you remember the painfully significant memories but also many other incredible memories too. The times where you think, "How on earth did I get there?"

Recollections of amazing times, hysterically funny times and times which were sweet *at that time*, but you're a different person now. One changes, with the seasons. In fact, I believe, one should!

In Harlem, I had a memory that made me rejoice at the fact that I was right where I wanted to be!

So, there I was, on the 30th floor of a project building. I was not going in and out of the lift, or elevator as it's called Stateside. You're chancing losing a couple of hours of your life every time you go into one of those lifts as they constantly break down; it's always hot (I mean roasting!) and I tended to find some form of bodily fluid every time I entered one. Either fresh blood, urine or more. You can grasp what I'm saying, I'm sure?

Anyhow, I used to run down the back stairwell of the building. I can run……fast. I can fly, if I decide to, straight over the banister rail. I didn't know what or who I was going to find in that stairwell, but I just preferred it. The stairwell stank! The usual bodily excrements were there also but I could fly past them couldn't I? There were lights broken so it was pitch black. It was likely I could run into an inebriated person possibly high on heroin. Or someone waiting with a knife. Or a rapist. The staff regularly experienced these situations.

But when you trust in the covering of the Lord, have you got the right or the time to worry?

God needed someone to reach the children living in those buildings. He needed someone to tell them, "I love you; I care about you and so does Jesus." So, there I am, running swiftly down the stairwell, ready to the next floor or two flights down.

AND I REMEMBERED!

It was a split second thought………..

Me! On another staircase. The most exquisite of staircases, in the Hotel du Paris in Monte Carlo.

I instantly, in that split second thought, encountered a memory that was much longer than a split second. But that's the power of our minds! We can remember so much, in such a short time span!

Whilst physically running down a dim stairwell in New York City, I was mentally transported to Monte Carlo. I was sitting on the third step from the bottom of the most splendid staircase. The wood had the most elegant and polished of carvings, and the atmosphere was a feeling of being enveloped in the most potent and provocative way. I was wearing a beautiful black evening gown and the gentleman I was with was on one knee. Yes. He was proposing to me with a ring that we had looked at earlier in the week. Hey! Believe me when I say I was not planning on my window shopping being any more than that! We had just enjoyed a meal in the Louis XV restaurant in the Hotel de Paris and I was feeling slightly heady with my intake of pink champagne. The man I had previously thought I had fallen in love with was about to propose. He was a very wealthy man and at that time was applying for residency in Monte Carlo. He knew that I was trying to end our 'friendship' as I had discovered his sworn declaration of love for me and for my God were empty words and I had finally accepted I was worth more and that God had a plan for me, and it wouldn't be with this worldly man. Wealth, in a monetary fashion, means little to me, and to walk away was very easy. But I did hope that this man would one day truly love God and understand that a real relationship with Jesus would fill his life with more joy than any money ever could.

This whole episode taught me I could only ever commit and submit to a man who puts God first!

But for a while, I had an option of choosing a life where I would have, in secular terms, the essence of all that matters. Monetary wealth and houses and diamonds and trips whenever I liked and a possible home in the Caribbean, with a penthouse in the apartment blocks being built through one of his businesses. It truly was what some would see as a fairy tale.

But there are no such things as real life fairy tales and even though these situations can seem remarkably appealing, I can only settle for anything marked by God.

I am, in God, one of the richest women in the world!

And it was in that split second, in the Harlem stairwell, that I realised I wouldn't have wanted to be anywhere else in all the world!

There isn't anything that can Ellie'vate any of us more than knowing we are right where God needs us most! Making a difference in this world. Being where we are needed. Pouring out His love to those who are so very thirsty.

I knocked on a burgundy red door and shouted out, "It's Yogi Bear." That's how the residents and children would know it was a Metro World Child worker in the New York boroughs. A man answered in his vest and poked his head around the door. A strong stench came through. I could hear a woman screeching and a television was blaring out so loud. A child was screaming and crying. A baby was naked and crawling and tried to push through to see who it was. I gave the man the Sidewalk Sunday School leaflet and tried to chat with him and I knelt down to the baby and smiled.

I said, "Hello little one, oh, I just love you!" I explained what was happening within the next week and that hopefully we would see the kids soon at the meeting. A place and time where we could lavish love upon them.

Then I ran back to the stairwell.

In Harlem.

Give me Harlem over Monte Carlo. Any day!

Read ~ John 14:26, Haggai 2:3, Psalm 112:6

Ellie'vation ~ Find out about a charity and see if you can get involved by volunteering or speaking at venues for them to raise funds or even donating to them. Find out all about the vision and how the charity was founded. Catch the vision!

Day 39

Let it go

Today let's chat about that resentment you might be holding inside towards someone. I know, todays devotional is going to be a toughie! But what's the point of us meditating on our thoughts if we don't become a better person because of it? What's the point of reading my Bible if I don't become more like Jesus? What's the point of walking through the whole of this life if I don't end it being a person who made a difference, left a legacy, helped others enjoy their days on this beautiful earth?

Years ago, I decided to get rid of any and all resentment I held inside. The thing was, I didn't even know what I was letting myself in for! It was when I first found my faith many, many years ago, and I learned about forgiveness and unforgiveness.

Wow!

When I started to unravel the deep-rooted pain I had carried inside me and followed Jesus' example of forgiveness, it was then I understood how much resentment and bitterness we can hold towards the people who have hurt us, let us down, betrayed us and abused us. These three things are all tied up together and even though your reasons for feeling that way are probably completely legitimate, how long are you going to allow resentment to continue travelling with you on your journey?

It's not the best travelling companion, is it?

But life is a process; a journey of transformation if you choose. If you are willing, you can remove all resentment, all unforgiveness and all bitterness from your life. If you turn to Jesus and ask Him to help you, I can assure you He will. Due to events I had experienced when I was younger I had so much I needed help with, and let me tell you now, I don't have one tiny iota of unforgiveness towards anyone, for any of the pain they caused me.

Forgiving people sets you free! Forgiving people removes resentment! Forgiving people eliminates bitterness!

Ellie'vate yourself today!

Say a prayer and ask God to help you forgive. He will. I promise! It may take time, or it could be swift, but He will help you because it's His will that you forgive.

You can do this!

Read ~ Proverbs 10:12, Luke 15:11-32, Job 36:13

Ellie'vation ~ Write a poem. If you haven't ever done this before and you think you can't, I challenge you! You can do this! Write a poem. Just take some paper and a pen and write down the first thing that comes to mind. See what happens! You could end up writing a whole book of poems!

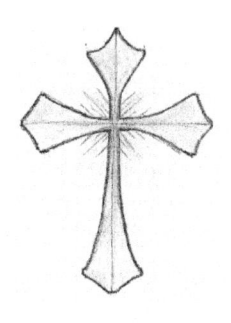

Day 40

Celebrate Bravery

I am brave.

It's such a simple statement but it's true. Why do I believe that I am brave?

When I was a young child, I would climb trees and swing from ropes and float on pieces of wood across dangerous expanses of water. I would ride my bike without wondering if a car was going to hit me. I wouldn't ever walk anywhere really because I would handstand all the way and commence with forward rolls along the pavement. I would play outside late into the evening and as a Brownie I would do odd jobs in stranger's houses to gain badges to sew onto my dress.

None of these things were brave. They were naïve acts, and I was young. I have always had an adventurous spirit, a daring spirit, an impulsive spirit. It's not necessarily brave to be any of these things. Riding around on the back of my boyfriend's motorbike screaming,

"Faster, faster," wasn't brave. Jumping from the top of huge waterfalls in India wasn't brave. Swimming with sharks wasn't brave. Adventurous, but not particularly brave.

I believe that I, and so many others are brave, because we ask God to use us.

Well, what's so brave about that, you may wonder?

Try it. Ask God to use you. And see what happens.

We live in a world where God needs people to get out on the frontline for Him. He needs brave people who aren't afraid of ridicule, who aren't terrified of being unpopular, who aren't horrified at the concept of upsetting people because they are God pleasers, not people pleasers!

When did we last ask God to use us as a vessel to save a soul? When did we last ask God to use us to kindle revival in our community, our church, our home? When did we last ask God, "What do YOU want ME to do for YOU?"

Every day I live for God, and I know many do, yet it can seem as if life itself takes over and we're busy being busy.

But bravery specifies a cause and a purpose larger than only yourself. If this is illuminated anywhere it's when we look at the example of Jesus Christ and the bravery He showed as He went to the Cross to give His life in exchange for ours, dying for our sins, so that we could have eternal life with our Father in heaven.

Now, I realise, I am not as brave as I like to think.

Yes, I will be a fool for my God. Yes, I will run up and down stairs in the project buildings of Harlem, New York, where the rapes and murders take place, because I want to reach the children with the Gospel. Yes, I will go out into the streets of the UK to reach the homeless and the street girls on dark, rainy nights to feed them. Yes, I will tell prisoners in a jail, some of whom spit and swear, that Jesus loves them.

I am brave. But only because He was braver.

Let's Ellie'vate His Name today.

And every day.

Read ~ Joshua 1:6-9, 1 Chronicles 28:20, Psalm 27:14

Ellie'vate ~ Do a study of every scripture in the Bible that speaks of courage. Meditate on these. Remind yourself that in Christ you are always strong, always brave!

Also available by Ellie Palma-Cass.

"I was absolutely riveted......"

"This is an astonishing testimony of a survivor....."

"This book delivers a punch for righteousness in the face of adversity!"

www.elliepalmacass.com

Printed in Great Britain
by Amazon